REVERSIBLE KNITTING

50 Brand-New, Groundbreaking Stitch Patterns

+**20** PROJECTS FROM TOP DESIGNERS

LYNNE BARR

PHOTOGRAPHY BY THAYER ALLYSON GOWDY

STC Craft/A Melanie Falick Book | Stewart Tabori & Chang | New York

Published in 2009 by Stewart, Tabori & Chang
An imprint of Harry N. Abrams, Inc.

Library of Congress Cataloging-in-Publication Data:
Barr, Lynne.
Reversible knitting / Lynne Barr ; photography by Thayer Allyson Gowdy.
p. cm.
ISBN 978-1-58479-805-7
1. Knitting--Patterns. I. Title.

TT825.B2978 2009
746.43'2--dc22

2008049039

Editor: Melanie Falick
Designer: Onethread
Production Manager: Jacqueline Poirier

Wardrobe Stylist: www.stylistjasmine.com
Hair and Makeup: Brynn for ArtistUnited.com
Models: Ellen/Ford SF and Heather S./Look Model Agency
Prop Stylist: Leigh Noe

The text of this book was composed in Din Schrift and Scala.

Printed and bound in China
10 9 8 7 6 5 4 3 2 1

harry n. abrams, inc.
a subsidiary of La Martinière Groupe

115 West 18th Street
New York, NY 10011
www.hnabooks.com

table of contents

introduction

After I finished my first book, *Knitting New Scarves,* I didn't know if I would write another knitting book. But when my editor mentioned the possibility of creating a book of new reversible stitch patterns and projects, I was intrigued. Certainly, I had thought about reversibility while I was working on the scarf book since reversibility is a relevant issue when creating scarves, but I wondered at first if I could come up with enough reversible stitch patterns to fill a book without relying on those that already appeared in other places. Once I realized that I could achieve that goal, I took on the challenge and began designing stitch patterns and projects and also invited other designers whose work I admired to contribute their own reversible projects. While I knew that I would base most of my projects on the stitch patterns I was developing, I did not ask the other designers to use them because I wanted to extend the offerings of this book beyond my own skills and style inclinations. I'm sure when you turn to the project section that begins on page 92 you will be as impressed with and intrigued by the diversity of their offerings as I am.

It may be human nature to play to one's strengths, but I find that working through a weakness or facing an obstacle often sparks my creative development. This is definitely how I approached the creation of stitches for this book. This may be most evident in several stitches from the Faux Crochet series (see page 7). Since I lack crochet skills beyond the simple crochet chain, I marveled at what crochet could do, and wondered how I could emulate that with knitting. Many crochet stitches appeared to be, at least from my inexperienced perspective, individual little decorative units tethered to each other by chains across great expanses of open space. With knitting needles and yarn in hand, I kept asking myself, "How do I get there from here?" When it dawned on me that a length of crochet chain looks like a column of knit stitches, the YOC was born, and this new revelation set me free. YOC is my name for the Yarnover Chain technique (see page 189), an inherently simple sequence with far-reaching possibilities.

To further challenge myself, I decided to impose two technical constraints while creating these stitches. The first was that each row of a stitch pattern had to end without leaving even a single double-pointed needle dangling in its wake. I set this requirement partly in response to some of the scarf patterns in *Knitting New Scarves,* which relied on numerous double-pointed needles being used in unconventional ways to create three-dimensional shapes. Many of the stitches in *Reversible Knitting* also work in three dimensions, but since these patterns may be destined for pieces much larger than a scarf, it seemed unreasonable to ask knitters to complete each repeat with stitches left on more than one needle. Otherwise, the number of needles would multiply with the number of repeats across the row and could become unwieldy.

My second self-imposed constraint was that neither attachment of new yarns, nor cutting and reattaching would be allowed. Shaping or embellishment had to be created from one continuous length of yarn. This also extended from the stitch patterns to the One-Run Socks (see page 166) and Tie Socks (see page 162), where I incorporated straps, ties, and bands all worked in one continuous run from the top to the toe.

Left to right: Transformation of the Folded Cables stitch (see page 26) into the Branching Ribs scarf (see page 96).

All the stitches in this book can be worked exactly as written, but to encourage you to use them as creative inspiration for your own unique designs, I modified the stitch patterns when I used them for my own finished garments and accessories. For two simple modifications, I slightly enlarged the Folded Fabric stitch (see page 75), adapting it to work in the round for the Folded Mini Dress (see page 118). For the Folded Scarf (see page 94), I expanded the same stitch into a scarf with a generous width.

An example of a more extreme modification is the transformation of the Folded Cables stitch into the Branching Ribs scarf (see above). I reached the final design after two modifications to the original stitch. Initially, I worked an enlarged single repeat, but couldn't expand the cable far enough to get the scarf width I wanted. So I made a big leap to the second version, in which I created two parallel folds worked in Stockinette and reverse Stockinette, and then disconnected them from adjacent stitches, allowing them to flutter freely. It still didn't feel quite right to me, so to reduce the flutter, I added short rows and changed entirely to rib.

Ultimately, my goal in writing this book is to add something different to the stitch pattern references that many knitters may already own, and offer exciting new patterns with a reversible twist. And as with *Knitting New Scarves*, I hope that what I offer here are some new ways of looking at knitting that will inspire you to explore and create unique designs of your own.

CROCHET
FAUX

FAUX CROCHET

STITCHES

01~09

For these stitch patterns I looked to crochet for inspiration. My intention was not to displace crochet, but to discover new ways of knitting and to push perceived boundaries. I had read that crochet was freer than knitting because it can be worked in all directions–horizontal, vertical, and every compass direction in between–unlike knitting, which is typically worked horizontally across each row. In particular, Tilted (#04), Linked Disks (#05), and Triangles (#08) are my attempt to take advantage of that same freedom with knitting.

| A SIDE | B SIDE |

01 LOOPS

To vary the pattern shown and to create a fabric with more of a striped appearance, you could shorten the loops (by shortening the chains) and work extra rows of rib between them. For an even more dramatic variation, you could create a highly textured checkerboard pattern by alternating squares of loops with squares of plain rib.

STITCH AND ROW INFORMATION
Even number of sts; 10-row repeat.

NOTE
Requires 2 additional circular (circ) needles or double-pointed needles (dpn) the same size as working needles, and a crochet hook.

Row 1 (A): *K1, p1; repeat from * to end.
Rows 2-8: Repeat Row 1.

Divide sts onto 2 circ needles or dpns as follows: Slip knit sts to front needle and purl sts to back needle.
Row 9: With crochet hook, work knit sts on front needle as follows: Slip first st to crochet hook, yarn over hook and draw through st on hook, *chain 14, slip next st from front needle to hook, yarn over hook and draw through both loops on hook; repeat from * to end. Transfer last loop from crochet hook to left-hand end of back needle, being careful not to twist st.
Row 10: K2tog, *with left-hand needle, pick up purl st at base of crocheted loop and purl it, k1; repeat from * to last st, k1-f/b.
Repeat Rows 1-10 for Loops.

02 BASIC FAUX CROCHET

To help make this stitch usable in many patterns, I decided it was important to anchor it to a commonly used stitch pattern. And so, knit 1, purl 1 rib is the foundation of Basic Faux Crochet, allowing this stitch to be easily substituted or incorporated into patterns that use this rib.

STITCH AND ROW INFORMATION

Multiple of 2 sts (st count varies through pattern), 6-row repeat.

NOTES

1) This st pattern looks identical on both sides. 2) Requires st holder and 1 additional needle 3 sizes larger than working needles for CO row and Row 5. 3) When knitting or purling a yo from a previous row, work it so that you create a hole (see Open the Yarnover, page 189).

ABBREVIATION

P2B (pick up 2 below): Pick up 2 sts in next available hole as follows: Insert right-hand needle from front to back through hole, wrap yarn around needle and bring forward through hole (see photo 2), insert right-hand needle from back to front through same hole, wrap yarn around needle and bring backward through hole (see photo 3).

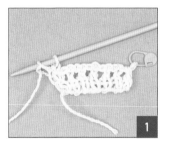

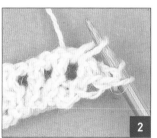

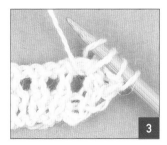

CO sts with larger needle. Change to smaller needles.

Rows 1 and 2: Slip 1 knitwise, *p1, k1; repeat from * to last st, p1.

Row 3: Slip 1 knitwise, p1, *yo, skp; repeat from * to end.

Row 4: Transfer 1 st to st holder, BO sts knitwise until 1 st remains on left-hand needle, p1 [2 sts remain on needle, 1 on st holder (see photo 1)].

Row 5: Change to larger needle. Slip 1 knitwise, p1, *P2B; repeat from * to end, k1 from st holder.

Row 6: Change to smaller needles. K2tog, *p1, k1; repeat from * to last st, p1.

Repeat Rows 1-6 for Basic Faux Crochet.

03 FAUX CROCHET BOBBLES

I developed this stitch pattern after the Basic Faux Crochet (page 9), and it is also compatible with a knit 1, purl 1 rib. After completing either Row 1 or Row 4, simply eliminate the yarnovers in Rows 2 or 5 and you will have transitioned to a knit 1, purl 1 rib.

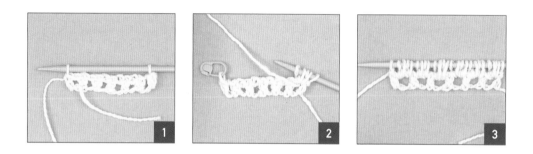

STITCH AND ROW INFORMATION
Odd number of sts (st count varies through pattern); 6-row repeat.

NOTES
1) This st pattern looks identical on both sides. 2) Requires st holder. 3) CO sts loosely, or use a needle 1 or 2 sizes larger.

ABBREVIATION
P4B (pick up 4 below): Pick up 4 sts in next available hole as follows: *Insert right-hand needle from front to back through hole, wrap yarn around needle and bring forward through hole, bring yarn to front, insert right-hand needle from back to front through same hole, wrap yarn around needle and bring backward through hole, bring yarn to back; repeat from * once. *Note: Make sure sts are picked up very loosely. If picked-up sts are tight, use a needle 1-2 sizes larger than working needles to pick up the sts.*

Set-Up Row 1: K1, *yo, skp; repeat from * to end.
Set-Up Row 2: K1, BO sts knitwise (beginning with last 2 sts worked) until 1 st remains at each end of right-hand needle (see photo 1).
Rows 1 and 4: Slip 1, transfer last st on left-hand needle to st holder, *P4B (see photo 2); repeat from * to end, k1 from st holder (see photo 3).
Row 2: Slip 1, [k1, p1] twice, *yo, [k1, p1] twice; repeat from * to last st, k1.
Row 3: Slip 2 wyib, p3tog, pso, *p1, pso, slip 1 wyib, p3tog, p2so; repeat from * to last st, k1, pso–1 st remains at each end of needle.
Row 5: Slip 1, *yo, [k1, p1] twice; repeat from * to last st, yo, k1.
Row 6: Slip 1, p1, slip 1 wyib, p3tog, p2so, *p1, pso, slip 1 wyib, p3tog, p2so; repeat from * to last 2 sts, p1, pso, k1, pso–1 st remains at each end of needle.
Repeat Rows 1–6 for Faux Crochet Bobbles.

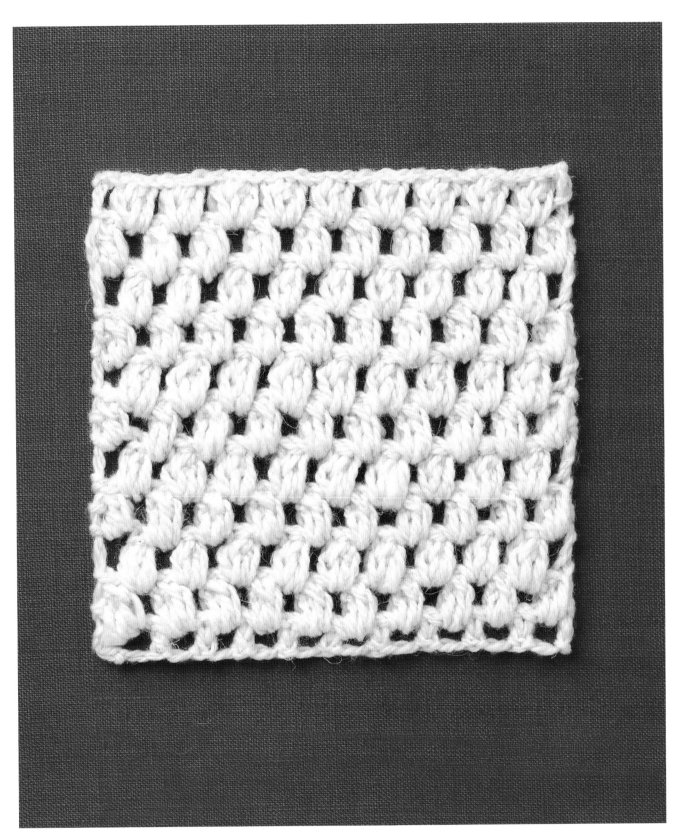

TILTED

When I first began designing this stitch pattern I worked all of the tilted boxes as lace, since visually, the open-worked boxes best supported the crochet-inspired theme. Ultimately, I changed every other row to garter boxes, providing some contrast to the lace rows and delivering a more interesting pattern.

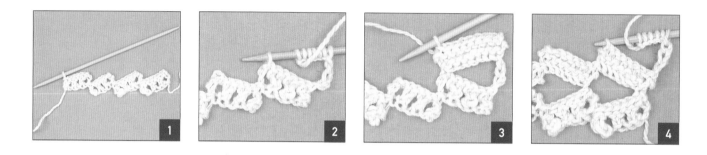

STITCH AND ROW INFORMATION

7 sts at CO (st count varies through pattern; 7 sts per Lace Box, 8 sts per Garter Box); 2-row repeat.

NOTES

1) The reverse side of this st pattern is a mirror image of the side shown. 2) Set-Up Rows 1-4 create the first Lace Box. For each additional Box needed, these rows must be repeated. Once you reach the desired width or number of Boxes, you will no longer work Set-Up Rows 1-4, but will work Pattern Rows instead. 3) When working Pattern Rows, each Box in the row is worked one at a time, so you will complete each new Box before moving on to the next Box in the row. 4) Garter Boxes are worked from left to right and Lace Boxes are worked from right to left. 5) When knitting or purling a yo from a previous row, work it so that you create a hole (see Open the Yarnover, page 189).

CO 7 sts.
Set-Up Rows 1 and 3: Knit.
Set-Up Row 2: K1, [yo, k2tog] 3 times.
Set-Up Row 4: BO 6 sts knitwise–1 st remains.
Additional Tilted Lace Boxes
*AO-f 6 sts. Repeat Set-Up Rows 1-4. Repeat from * to desired width or number of Lace Boxes (photo 1 shows Set-Up repeats).

Begin Pattern Rows
Row 1 (Tilted Garter Boxes): K1, yoc4, *AO-f 6 sts, wyif pick up 1 st from upper left-hand corner of Lace Box (see photo 2); [turn, k8] 3 times; turn, BO 7 sts knitwise–1 st remains (see photo 3). Repeat from * for remaining Boxes.
Row 2 (Tilted Lace Boxes): K1, yoc4, *AO-f 5 sts, wyif pick up 1 st from upper left-hand corner of Garter Box (see photo 4); turn, k7; turn, k1, [yo, k2tog] 3 times; turn, k7; turn, BO 6 sts knit-wise–1 st remains. Repeat from * for remaining Boxes.
Repeat Pattern Rows 1 and 2 for Tilted. Cut yarn and pull through last st to fasten off.

05 LINKED DISKS

My intention with this stitch pattern was to create the illusion of seemingly unconnected disks, floating with almost invisible support. In order to work from one disk to the next, I devised the YOC (Yarnover Chain; see page 189), which allowed me to move from disk to disk and from row to row with only minimal contact.

STITCH AND ROW INFORMATION

Multiple of 18 sts + 1 at CO (st count varies through pattern); 1-row repeat.

NOTES

1) The reverse side of this st pattern is a mirror image of the side shown. 2) Do not hide wraps.

Row 1: Slip 1, *k7, w&t; k6, w&t; k5, w&t; k4, w&t; k3, w&t; k2, w&t; k5, slip last st back to left-hand needle, k2tog, k1, [k1, pso] 7 times, slip last st back to left-hand needle, k2tog; repeat from * to end.

Row 2: Slip 1, yoc2, *yoc3, AO-f 8 sts; work these 8 sts as follows: slip 1 wyib, k6, w&t; k5, w&t; k4, w&t; k3, w&t; k2, w&t; k4, k1-f/b, yoc3, slip last st to left-hand needle, k2tog, [k1, pso] 7 times, slip last st back to left-hand needle, k2tog; repeat from * to end.

Repeat Row 2 for Linked Disks, end final repeat of Row 2 by working yoc5 from last st.

BO Set-Up Row: Slip 1 st to right-hand needle, *AO-f 8 sts, k9; repeat from * to end of row.

BO all sts knitwise.

06 GARTER LATTICE

While working on this stitch pattern, I was inspired to learn to purl stitches from the right-hand needle onto the left-hand needle so that I would be able to work the Garter sections without having to turn my work. It turned out to be a relatively easy task.

2 sts at CO (st count varies through pattern); 2-row repeat.

NOTE
The reverse side of this st pattern is a mirror image of the side shown.

CO Row: CO 2 sts. K1, k1-f/b, *yoc2, slip last st knitwise to left-hand needle, k1-f/b/f; repeat from * until row is approximately 1" short of desired width, end last repeat k1-f/b instead of k1-f/b/f.
Row 1: [K2, turn] 6 times, *k1, k1-f/b, yoc5, slip last st knitwise to left-hand needle, k2tog, k1, [turn, k2] 5 times, turn; repeat from * to end, end last repeat [turn, k2] 4 times instead of [turn, k2] 5 times.
Row 2: [K2, turn] 6 times, *k1, k1-f/b, yoc2, slip last st knitwise to left-hand needle, k2tog, k1, [turn, k2] 5 times, turn; repeat from * to end, end last repeat [turn, k2] 4 times instead of [turn, k2] 5 times.
Repeat Rows 1 and 2 for Garter Lattice.
BO Row: BO 1 st, *yoc2, BO 2 sts; repeat from * to end.
Cut yarn and pull through last st to fasten off.

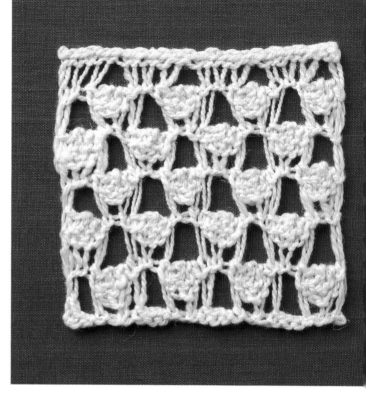

07 LITTLE DISKS

This stitch pattern came about while I was playing with the technique of Increasing in Wrapped Stitches (see page 187). When an elongated wrapped stitch is placed next to an ordinary knit stitch, the elongation is accentuated and a curved shape is created. The increases in the wraps produce enough stitches to shape the little disks with short rows. The result reminds me of rows of flower buds.

STITCH AND ROW INFORMATION

Multiple of 6 sts + 1 (st count varies through pattern); 4-row repeat.

NOTES

1) The reverse side of this st pattern is a mirror image of the side shown. 2) Do not hide wraps.

Set-Up Row: K1-wy2, *[k1-wy3] twice, k1, [k1, pso] twice, k1-wy3, pso; repeat from * to end.

Rows 1 and 3: *Kw-f/b, AO-f 1 st; repeat from * to last st, k1, dropping extra wrap.

Row 2: K1-wy2, *k5, w&t; k4, w&t; k3, w&t; [k2tog] twice, turn; slip 1 st wyib, k1, pso, k2tog, pso, k1-wy3, pso, [k1-wy3] twice; repeat from * to end.

Row 4: K1-wy2, *[k1-wy3] twice, k5, w&t; k4, w&t; k3, w&t; [k2tog] twice, turn; slip 1 wyib, k1, pso, k2tog, pso, k1-wy3, pso; repeat from * to end.

Repeat Rows 1-4 for Little Disks, ending with Row 2 or 4.

BO Set-Up Row: Work Row 1 or 3, omitting all AO-f sts. BO all sts knitwise.

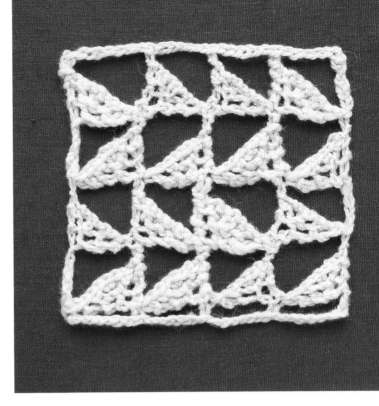

08 TRIANGLES

This open geometric look is very unusual for a stitch pattern, but knitting and connecting these simple triangles is really quite easy.

STITCH AND ROW INFORMATION

7 sts per Triangle, 1 st at CO (st count varies through pattern); 1-row repeat.

NOTES

1) The reverse side of this st pattern is a mirror image of the side shown. 2) After working Set-Up Row, the number of sts on the needle is one greater than the number of Triangles you will have after working Row 1. 3) Each Triangle in Row 1 is worked one at a time, so you will complete each new Triangle before moving on to the next Triangle in the row. 4) When knitting or purling a yo from a previous row, work it so that you create a hole (see Open the Yarnover, page 189).

ABBREVIATION

WT (Work Triangle): K1, yo, k1, turn; k3, turn; k1, [yo, k1] twice, turn; k5, turn; k1, [yo, k1] 4 times, turn; k2, [k1, pso] 7 times.

CO 1 st.

Set-Up Row: *K1-f/b, yoc6, slip last st to left-hand needle; repeat from * to end, ending final repeat after working yoc6.

Row 1: K1, slip last st back to left-hand needle, k1-f/b, *turn, WT, k1 from next needle**, [turn, k2] twice; repeat from * to end, end final repeat at **, pso, yoc4.

Repeat Row 1 for Triangles.

BO Row: K1-f/b, *pso, yoc6, k1; repeat from * to end, pso. Cut yarn and pull through last st to fasten off.

09 TWIST

This is an easy little drop-stitch pattern… with a twist. If you want to make increases in this pattern and still keep all the twists vertically lined up from row to row, then you need to make the increases at the side edge. To add one new multiple (3 stitches) to a side, k1-f/b in the edge stitch on Rows 4-6.

Multiple of 3 sts (st count varies through pattern); 6-row repeat.

NOTE
This st pattern looks identical on both sides.

CO a minimum of 6 sts.
Row 1: *K1-wy3; repeat from * to end.
Row 2: *Slip 3 sts purlwise wyib, dropping extra wraps, insert left-hand needle, from right to left, into front of 3 slipped sts, k3tog, yo; repeat from * to end, end last repeat k3tog, instead of k3tog, yo.
Row 3: K1-b/f/b, *k1, k1-b/f; repeat from * to end.
Rows 4-6: Knit.
Repeat Rows 1-6 for Twist.

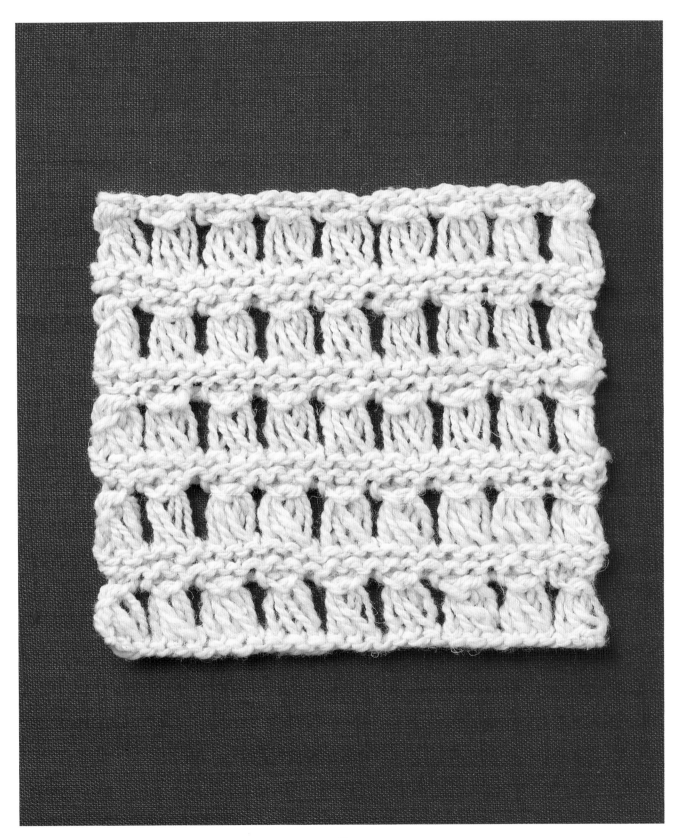

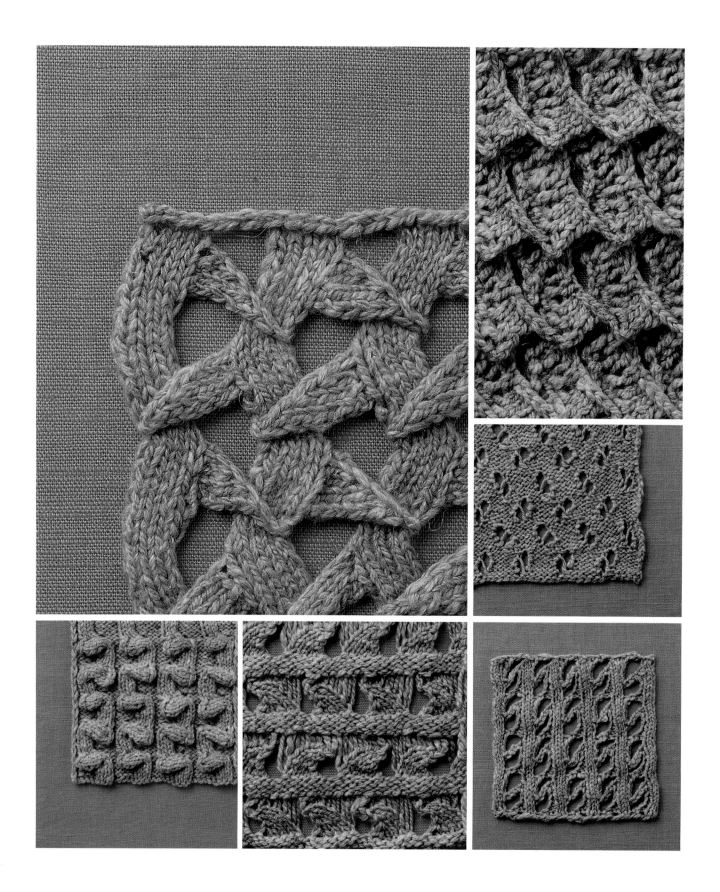

ROWS WITHIN ROWS

STITCHES
10~18

Rows Within Rows is a natural successor to the Faux Crochet section, which led me away from knitting in a strictly horizontal direction across each row. For these stitch patterns, each multiple of the pattern that is cast on is worked vertically for several rows before moving on to the next multiple in the pattern row. Unlike traditional stitch patterns, which develop slowly row by row, these patterns develop almost complete motifs within a single row.

10A Deconstructed Stockinette
11B Lacy "S" Rib
12A Flags
13A Folded Cables
14A Surf
17B No-Wrap Short Rows

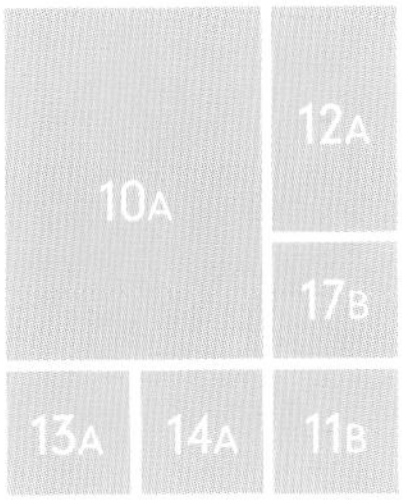

10 DECONSTRUCTED STOCKINETTE

I can imagine this stitch used as a vertical decorative insert traveling up the front and back of a Stockinette-stitch vest, or worked horizontally along a lower portion of a sweater body or sleeve.

A SIDE   B SIDE

STITCH AND ROW INFORMATION

Multiple of 5 sts (st count varies through pattern); 2-row repeat.

NOTES

1) Cable needle (cn) is optional. You may avoid using the cn if you open the stitch a little when you slip it from the needle, then pull the stitch snug after slipping it back to the left-hand needle. 2) When slipping a st at the beginning of the row, if the next st to be worked is a knit st, slip the st wyib; if the next st is a purl st, slip the st wyif. 3) To work a yo(beg), follow directions for Beginning of Row Yarnover (see page 189). 4) When knitting or purling a yo from a previous row, work it so that you close the hole (see Close the Yarnover, page 189).

CO a minimum of 10 sts.

Set-Up Row (B): Purl.

Row 1: Slip 1, k4, turn; slip 1, p4, turn;
slip 1, k4, *turn; yo(beg), p5, turn;
slip 1, k4, yo, k1, turn; slip 1, p1, yo, p5, turn;
slip 1, k4, yo, k3, turn; slip 1, p3, yo, p5, turn;
slip 1, k9, turn; slip 1, p4, turn;
k2tog-tbl, k3, turn; slip 1, p3, turn;
k2tog-tbl, k2, turn; slip 1, p2, turn;
k2tog-tbl, k1, turn; p2tog, turn;

slip first st on left-hand needle to cn and hold to front, slip next 5 sts to right-hand needle, slip st from cn to left-hand needle, wyif slip 1 from right-hand needle to left-hand needle, k2tog-tbl, [turn; slip 1, p4, turn; slip 1, k4] twice. Repeat from * to end, end final repeat [turn; slip 1, p4, turn; slip 1, k4] 3 times.

Row 2: Slip 1, p4, turn; slip 1, k4, turn;
slip 1, p4, *turn; yo(beg), k5, turn;
slip 1, p4, yo, p1, turn; slip 1, k1, yo, k5, turn;
slip 1, p4, yo, p3, turn; slip 1, k3, yo, k5, turn;
slip 1, p9, turn; slip 1, k2, k2tog, turn;
slip 1, p3, turn; slip 1, k1, k2tog, turn;
slip 1, p2, turn; slip 1, k2tog, turn;
p2tog, turn; slip first st on left-hand needle to cn and hold to front, slip next 5 sts from right-hand needle to left-hand needle, slip st from cn to left-hand needle, k2tog, k4, turn;
slip 1, p4, turn; slip 1, k4, turn;
slip 1, p4. Repeat from * to end, end final repeat [turn; slip 1, p4, turn; slip 1, k4] 2 more times, turn; slip 1, p4.

Repeat Rows 1 and 2 for Deconstructed Stockinette.

BO Row: Slip 1, [k1, pso] 4 times, *yoc3, slip 1, pso, [k1, pso] 4 times; repeat from * to end. Cut yarn and pull through last st to fasten off.

A SIDE

B SIDE

11 LACY "S" RIB

This was one of the first reversible stitch patterns I created, and it established "rows within rows" as a category for this book. With it I realized that knitting connected units didn't have to result in only simple-looking, blocky geometric shapes. I love this stitch pattern and intend to knit a long, long scarf using it.

STITCH AND ROW INFORMATION

Multiple of 4 sts + 2; 2-row repeat.

NOTES

1) This stitch pattern is easier to work on a circular needle.
2) When slipping a st at the beginning of the row, if the next st to be worked is a knit st, slip the st wyib; if the next st is a purl st, slip the st wyif. 3) Row 2, when completed, increases the knitting by 8 rows.

CO sts very loosely.

Row 1 (A): Slip 1 purlwise, p1, *k2; work previous 2 sts, as follows: [Turn, slip 1 purlwise, p1; turn, slip 1 knitwise, k1] twice, p2 from next needle; repeat from * to end.

Row 2: Slip 1 knitwise, k1, p2; work previous 4 sts as follows: [Turn, slip 1 knitwise, k1, p2] 8 times; work previous 2 sts: [Turn, slip 1 purlwise wyib, k1; turn, slip 1 purlwise, p1] 4 times. Do not turn. *Work 4 sts from next needle as follows: K2, p2; work previous 6 sts as follows: [Turn, slip 1 knitwise, k1, p2, k2; turn, slip 1 purlwise, p1, k2, p2] 4 times; work previous 2 sts as follows: [Turn, slip 1 purlwise wyib, k1; turn, slip 1 purlwise, p1] 4 times. Do not turn. Repeat from * to last 2 sts, k2; work previous 4 sts as follows: [Turn, slip 1 purlwise, p1, k2] 8 times.
Repeat Rows 1 and 2 for Lacy "S" Rib.

BO Row: P2, pso, *slip 1 st from right-hand needle to left-hand needle, k2tog, k1, [turn, slip 1 purlwise, p1; turn, slip 1 knitwise, k1] twice, pso, p2tog, pso; repeat from * until 1 st remains. Cut yarn and pull through last st to fasten off.

12 FLAGS

As a contrast to the more contemporary look of many of my other stitch patterns, I decided to create one with an almost baroque style. The three-dimensional laciness of this stitch pattern helps accomplish the ornate feeling I was after.

STITCH AND ROW INFORMATION

Multiple of 5 sts (st count varies through pattern); 4-row repeat.

NOTES

1) Cable needle (cn) is optional. You may avoid using the cn if you open the stitch a little when you slip it from the needle, then pull the stitch snug after slipping it back to the left-hand needle.
2) When knitting or purling a yo from a previous row, work it so that you create a hole (see Open the Yarnover, page 189).

ABBREVIATIONS

WF (Work Flag): K3, k2tog, yo, p1, turn; k2, yo, p4, turn; k2, k2tog, yo, p3, turn; k4, yo, p3, turn; k1, k2tog, yo, p5, turn; k6, yo, p2, turn; k2tog, yo, p4, [p1, pso] 3 times. Do not turn.

WLF (Work Last Flag): K3, k2tog, yo, p1, turn; k2, p4, turn; k2, k2tog, yo, p2, turn; k3, p3, turn; k1, k2tog, yo, p3, turn; k4, p2, turn; k2tog, p4.

CO a minimum of 15 sts.
Set-Up Row (A): Purl.
Row 1: K5, turn; yo, *p5, turn**; WF, slip last st worked to cn and hold to back, slip 5 sts from left-hand needle to right-hand needle, slip st from cn back to right-hand needle, turn; k1, yoc1; repeat from * to end, ending final repeat at **, WLF.
Row 2: *K2, k2tog, yo, p1; repeat from * to end.
Row 3: *K2, yo, p2tog, p1; repeat from * to end.
Row 4: *K2tog, yo, p3; repeat from * to end.
Repeat Rows 1-4 for Flags.

13 FOLDED CABLES

I created this stitch pattern after Turbulent Rib (page 28). I wanted to use the curved shape created by the short-rowed yarn-overs again, but in a non-lacy fabric with a different pattern on the reverse side.

STITCH AND ROW INFORMATION

Multiple of 9 sts + 3 at CO (st count varies through pattern); 14-row repeat.

NOTES

1) Requires 1 double-pointed needle (dpn) the same size as working needles. 2) Do not hide wraps.

Row 1 (A): P3, *k3, p2, p2-tbl, p2; repeat from * to end.
Rows 2, 4, and 6: *K6, p3; repeat from * to last 3 sts, k3.
Rows 3 and 5: P3, *k3, p6; repeat from * to end.
Row 7: P3, *[yo, k3, turn; slip 1 purlwise, p2, w&t] 3 times, k3, turn; with dpn, slip 1 purlwise, [p1, pso] 3 times, p2, turn; hold dpn to front, slip 3 from left-hand to right-hand needle, k3 from dpn, p3 from left-hand needle; repeat from * to end.
Row 8: K3, *p3, k2, [k1-tbl] twice, k2; repeat from * to end.
Rows 9, 11, and 13: *P6, k3; repeat from * to last 3 sts, p3.
Rows 10 and 12: K3, *p3, k6; repeat from * to end.
Row 14: K3, *[yo, p3, turn; slip 1 knitwise, k2, w&t] 3 times, p3, turn; with dpn, slip 1 knitwise, [k1, pso] 3 times, k2, turn; hold dpn to back, slip 3 from left-hand to right-hand needle, p3 from dpn, k3 from next needle; repeat from * to end.
Repeat Rows 1-14 for Folded Cables.

A SIDE   B SIDE

14 SURF

To use this stitch pattern in a project that requires shaping, plan increases for the rows of Reverse Stockinette stitch between the left curls on Rows 3 and the right curls on Row 8. Worked without shaping, I think this stitch pattern, done in a richly colored yarn, would make a beautiful lightweight scarf.

STITCH AND ROW INFORMATION
Multiple of 6 sts + 3; 10-row repeat.

NOTE
Work yo's before knit sts using Alternative method (see Alternative Yarnover, page 188).

ABBREVIATIONS
LC (Left Curl)
Yo4, k5, slip 1, turn; p2tog, p4, turn;
yo3, k4, slip 1, turn; p2tog, p3, turn;
yo3, k3, slip 1, turn; p2tog, p2, turn;
yo2, k2, slip 1, turn; p2tog, p1, turn;
yo2, k1, slip 1, turn; p2tog, turn; k1-wy2.

RC (Right Curl)
Yo4, p5, slip 1, turn; k2tog, k4, turn;
yo3, p4, slip 1, turn; k2tog, k3, turn;
yo3, p3, slip 1, turn; k2tog, k2, turn;
yo2, p2, slip 1, turn; k2tog, k1, turn;
yo2, p1, slip 1, turn; k2tog, turn; p1-wy2.

Rows 1, 5, and 7 (A): Purl.
Rows 2 and 6: Knit.
Row 3: *LC; repeat from * to last 3 sts, yo4, k2, slip 1, turn; p2tog, p1, turn; yo3, k1, slip 1, turn; p2tog, turn; k1-wy2.
Row 4: Knit, dropping extra loops.
Row 8: *RC; repeat from * to last 3 sts, yo4, p2, slip 1, turn; k2tog, k1, turn; yo3, p1, slip 1, turn; k2tog, turn; p1-wy2.
Row 9: Purl, dropping extra loops.
Row 10: Knit.
Repeat Rows 1-10 for Surf.

15 TURBULENT RIB

I started this stitch pattern by first visualizing little horn-of-plenty shapes. I found that I could achieve this look by mixing short rows, yarnovers, and decreases. The next logical step was to incorporate them into a rib pattern to keep the fabric reversible, and so the "horns" are worked into a knit 6, purl 6 rib.

STITCH AND ROW INFORMATION
Multiple of 10 sts + 4; 18-row repeat.

NOTES
1) On the opposite side of the swatch shown, the knit sts reverse to purl sts and the purl sts reverse to knit sts. 2) All slip sts are slipped purlwise. 3) Do not hide wraps. 4) If pattern is worked with only 14 sts, do not work the sts between asterisks on Row 13.

ABBREVIATIONS
KC (Knit Curve)
Yo, k5, turn; p2tog, p3, w&t (wrap yo);
yo, k4, turn; p2tog, p2, w&t;
yo, k3, turn; p2tog, p1, w&t;
yo, k2, turn; p2tog, w&t; k1.

PC (Purl Curve)
Yo, p5, turn; k2tog-tbl, k3, w&t;
yo, p4, turn; k2tog-tbl, k2, w&t;
yo, p3, turn; k2tog-tbl, k1, w&t;
yo, p2, turn; k2tog-tbl, w&t; p1.

Rows 1-3: Slip 1, p1, *k5, p5; repeat from * to last 2 sts, k2.
Rows 4 and 9: Slip 1, p1, *KC, p1-tbl, p4; repeat from * to last 2 sts, k2.
Rows 5-8 and 10-12: Repeat Row 1.
Row 13: Slip 1, p1, k5, *PC, k1-tbl, k4; repeat from * to last 7 sts, PC, k1-tbl, k1.
Rows 14-17: Repeat Row 1.
Row 18: Repeat Row 13.
Repeat Rows 1-18 for Turbulent Rib.

16 ROLLING WAVES RIB

This stitch pattern is similar to one I developed for Drifting Pleats, a project in my first book, *Knitting New Scarves*. This one, however, delivers little curved pleats rather than continuous pleats carried up the length of the fabric. Each little pleat in Rolling Waves Rib is completed within a single row, which makes it easier to work than Drifting Pleats.

STITCH AND ROW INFORMATION
Multiple of 16 sts + 12; 12-row repeat.

NOTE
Requires 2 double-pointed needles (dpn) the same size as working needles.

ABBREVIATION
MW (Make Wave): Slip next 3 sts to empty dpn, slip next 3 sts to a second dpn, fold second dpn clockwise behind and parallel to first dpn. With working needle, k1, p1 from first dpn, k1, p1 from second dpn, k1 from first dpn, p1 from second dpn. Turn and work previous 6 sts as follows: With empty dpn, slip 1 knitwise, [p1, k1] twice, w&t; rib 5 sts, turn; with empty dpn, slip 1 knitwise, p1, k1, w&t; rib 3 sts, turn; with empty dpn, slip 1 knitwise, w&t; p1, turn; with empty dpn, slip 1 knitwise, rib 5 sts, hiding wraps, turn.

Rows 1-5: *K1, p1; repeat from * to end.
Row 6 (A): K1, p1, *MW; hold dpn with Wave sts to front, with right-hand needle, k1, p1 from next needle, [k1, p1] 3 times from dpn (Wave sts), [k1, p1] 3 times from next needle; repeat from * to last 6 sts, [k1, p1] 3 times.
Rows 7-11: *K1, p1; repeat from * to end.
Row 12: *[K1, p1] 3 times, MW; hold dpn with Wave sts to front, with working needle, k1, p1 from next needle, [k1, p1] 3 times from dpn (Wave sts); repeat from * to last 2 sts, k1, p1.
Repeat Rows 1-12 for Rolling Waves Rib.

17 NO-WRAP SHORT ROWS

My goal for this stitch pattern was simplicity. I was pleased to find that a charming lace pattern could be created with straight Stockinette stitch worked in modular sections.

STITCH AND ROW INFORMATION

Multiple of 6 sts + 3; 2-row repeat.

Row 1 (A): *[K6, turn; p6] 3 times, turn; k6; repeat from * to last 3 sts, [k3, turn; p3] 3 times, turn; k3.

Row 2: *[P6, turn; k6] 3 times, turn; p6; repeat from * to last 3 sts, *[p3, turn; k3] 3 times, turn, p3.

Repeat Rows 1 and 2 for No-Wrap Short Rows.

18 LOOPING RIB

Often one idea begets another, and so the design for this stitch pattern grew out of Deconstructed Stockinette (page 22). Both stitch patterns employ a similar process of adding new stitches to a vertical column, with the new stitches connecting horizontally to the next column.

STITCH AND ROW INFORMATION
4 sts at CO (st count varies through pattern); 2-row repeat.

NOTES
1) Requires 1 double-pointed needle (dpn) the same size as working needles. 2) When knitting or purling a yo from a previous row, work it so that you close the hole (see Close the Yarnover, page 189). 3) All slip stitches are slipped knitwise.

CO Row: CO 4 sts. *Yo(beg), [k1, p1] twice, turn; slip 1, p1, k1, p1, yo, p1, turn;
slip 1, p1, yo, [k1, p1] twice, turn; slip 1, p1, k1, p1, yo, p1, k1, p1, turn;
slip 1, p1, [k1, p1] 3 times, turn; slip 1, p1, [k1, p1] 3 times, [turn, slip 1, p1, k1, p1] 4 times, turn.
Repeat from * for desired width, end final repeat [turn, slip 1, p1, k1, p1] 2 more times.

A SIDE

B SIDE

Row 1 (A): Slip 1, p1, k1, p1, *turn; yo, [k1, p1] twice, turn; slip 1, p1, k1, p1, yo, p1, turn; slip 1, p1, yo, [k1, p1] twice, turn; slip 1, p1, k1, p1, yo, p1, k1, p1, turn; slip 1, p1, [k1, p1] 3 times, turn; slip 1, p1, [k1, p1] 3 times, [turn, slip 1, p1, k1, p1] 4 times, turn; with dpn slip 1, p1, k1, p1, turn; hold dpn in back of next 4 sts, [k2tog (1 st from each needle), p2tog (1 st from each needle)] twice. Repeat from * to end of row, end final repeat [turn, slip 1, p1, k1, p1] 6 times.

Row 2: Work as for Row 1, but hold dpn to front of work (not back) when ribbing sts together.

Repeat Rows 1 and 2 for Looping Rib, end final repeat with Row 2.

BO Row: [Slip 1, p1, k1, p1, turn] 9 times, with dpn slip 1, p1, k1, p1, turn; hold dpn to back, [k2tog (1 st from each needle), p2tog (1 st from each needle)] twice, turn; *[slip 1, p1, k1, p1, turn] 10 times, with dpn slip 1, p1, k1, p1, turn; hold dpn in back of next 4 sts, [k2tog (1 st from each needle), p2tog (1 st from each needle)] twice; repeat from * to end. BO remaining sts in k1, p1 pattern.

One-Row Variation

After completing the CO Row and Row 1, repeat only Row 1 until desired length. This creates a more three-dimensional pattern that is the same on both sides (see photo below).

ONE-ROW VARIATION

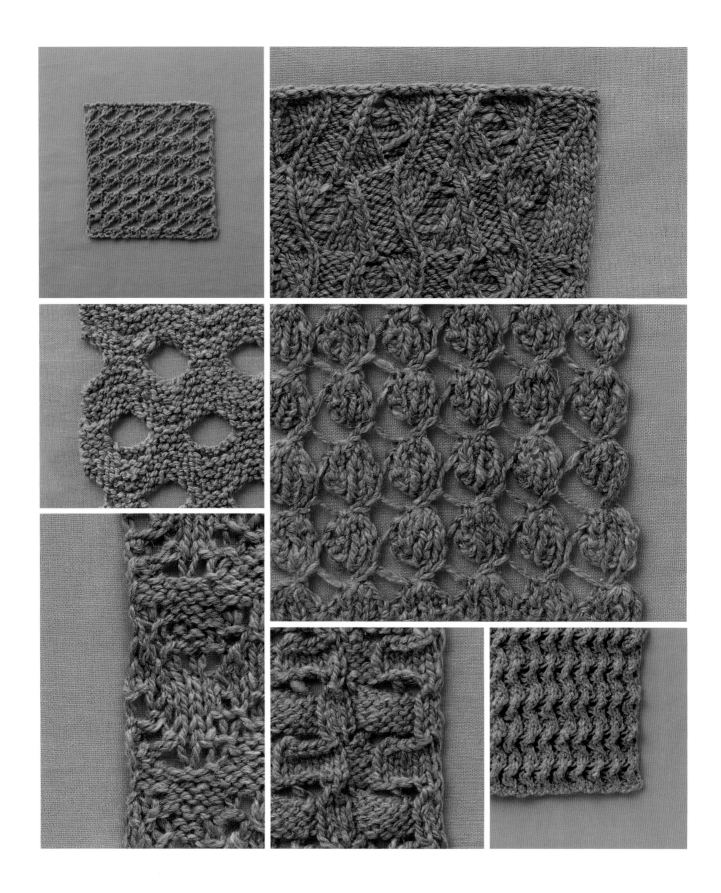

OPENWORK

OPENWORK

These stitches incorporate open space in the patterns through the traditional use of yarnovers, dropped stitches, and bind-offs followed by cast-ons. With the exception of Cabled Rib Cord (#19) and Half Nelson (#25), the stitches in this group are worked in the traditional direction from the first stitch in a row to the last, without turns or detours in other directions along the way. To create open space in Cabled Rib Cord, the cables are worked as short I-Cords, and for Half Nelson, simply knitting one small ribbed circle after another, like a knitted bobble fabric, creates the laciness of the stitch pattern.

19A	Cabled Rib Cord
20	Garter Lace Waves
22A	Cane Lace
23	Hills and Valleys
25	Half Nelson
26B	Dropped Stitches
27	Noyo Boxes

A SIDE

B SIDE

19 CABLED RIB CORD

For this stitch pattern, I used short I-cords, worked on Rows 2 and 5, to create open space in the fabric. I left this swatch compressed (unblocked), but blocking could be applied and the I-cords length-ened, creating a more open fabric.

STITCH AND ROW INFORMATION

Multiple of 4 sts + 2; 6-row repeat.

NOTE

Requires cable needle (cn).

Row 1 (A): Slip 1 purlwise, *k2, p2; repeat from * to last st, k1.
Row 2: Slip 1 purlwise, *k2, [slip 2 sts back to left-hand needle, k2] 3 times, p2; repeat from * to last st, k1.
Row 3: Slip 1 purlwise, *slip 2 sts to cn and hold to front, p2, k2 from cn; repeat from * to last st, k1.
Row 4: Slip 1 purlwise, *p2, k2; repeat from * to last st, k1.
Row 5: Slip 1 purlwise, *p2, k2, [slip 2 sts back to left-hand needle, k2] 3 times; repeat from * to last st, k1.
Row 6: Slip 1 purlwise, *slip 2 sts to cn and hold to back, k2, p2 from cn; repeat from * to last st, k1.
Repeat Rows 1-6 for Cabled Rib Cord.

20 GARTER LACE WAVES

Lacy wave patterns created through stacked yarnovers and decreases are not uncommon, but I wanted to create an open pattern that would feel bold rather than lacy. To minimize the feeling of lace, the yarnovers are knit closed to avoid holes, and all open space is confined between the waves.

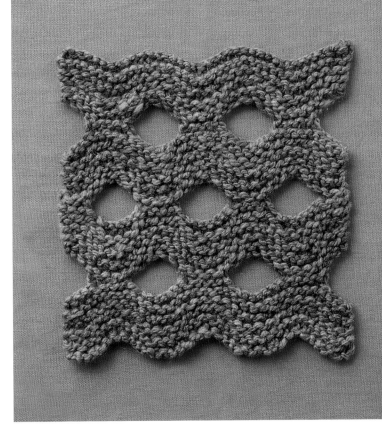

STITCH AND ROW INFORMATION

Multiple of 12 sts + 2 at CO (st count varies through pattern); 21-row repeat.

NOTES

1) This st pattern looks identical on both sides. 2) When knitting or purling a yo from a previous row, work it so that you close the hole (see Close the Yarnover, page 189). 3) When casting on additional sts, use Cable Cast-On (see page 178). 4) If pattern is worked with only 14 sts, do not work the sts between asterisks on Rows 10, 11, 20, and 21.

Rows 1, 4, and 7: K1, *[k2tog] twice, [k1, yo] 4 times, [k2tog] twice; repeat from * to last st, k1.
Rows 2, 3, 5, 6, and 8: Knit.
Row 9: BO 4 sts, knit to end.

Row 10: BO 4 sts, *k5, BO next 6 sts; repeat from * to last 5 sts, k5.
Row 11: CO 4 sts, knit these 4 sts, *k6, CO 6 sts; repeat from * to last 6 sts, k6, CO 4 sts.
Rows 12, 15, and 18: K1, *[k1, yo] twice, [k2tog] 4 times, [k1, yo] twice; repeat from * to last st, k1.
Rows 13, 14, 16, 17, and 19: Knit.
Row 20: K4, *BO next 6 sts, k5; repeat from * to last 10 sts, BO next 6 sts, k3.
Row 21: K4, *CO 6 sts, k6; repeat from * to last 4 sts, CO 6 sts, k4.
Repeat Rows 1-21 for Garter Lace Waves, ending final repeat with Row 19.
BO Set-Up Row: Knit 1 row.
BO all sts knitwise.

21 KNIT-ONLY LACE

This is a simple two-stitch, two-row pattern that is easy to shape. It is used in the One-Run Socks (page 166), which includes instructions for decreasing and increasing in pattern as well as converting to knitting in the round.

It is used in the One-Run Socks (page 166)

STITCH AND ROW INFORMATION
Even number of sts; 2-row repeat.

NOTE
This st pattern looks identical on both sides.

Row 1: *K1, k1-wy2; repeat from * to end.
Row 2: *Knit first wrap, dropping it from left-hand needle (see photo 1), insert tip of right-hand needle through remaining wrap purlwise (see photo 2), then into next st knitwise (without working wrap), pull st through wrap and knit it (see photo 3), drop wrap from left-hand needle (it will wrap loosely around st just knit, see photo 4); repeat from * to end.
Repeat Rows 1 and 2 for Knit-Only Lace, ending with Row 1.
BO Row: Working Row 2, BO all sts in pattern.

22 CANE LACE

Side A of this stitch pattern looks similar to the woven pattern seen in caned chairs. With only a three-stitch repeat, it's easier to shape than many lace patterns.

STITCH AND ROW INFORMATION

Multiple of 3 sts + 1 (st count varies through pattern); 4-row repeat.

Row 1 (A): P1, *k1, yo, k1, p1; repeat from * to end.
Row 2: K1, *p1, [p1, pso] twice, wyib slip 1 knitwise to left-hand needle, k2tog; repeat from * to end.
Row 3: P1, *yo, k1 into loop below next st on left-hand needle (see photos 1 and 2), p1; repeat from * to end.
Row 4: K1, *p2, k1; repeat from * to end.
Repeat Rows 1-4 for Cane Lace.

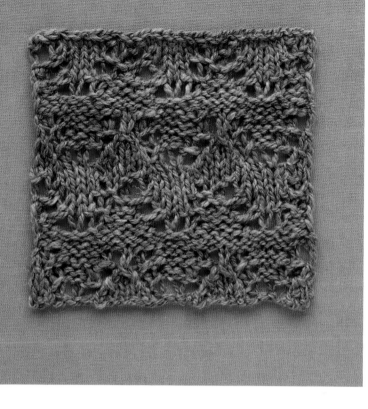

23 HILLS AND VALLEYS

Rather than using yarnovers, the typical method of creating holes for lace, I utilized increases made in multi-wrapped stitches to create an open network between the hills and valleys of this stitch pattern.

STITCH AND ROW INFORMATION

Multiple of 9 sts + 10 (st count varies through pattern); 7-row repeat.

NOTES

1) On the opposite side of the swatch shown, the knit sts reverse to purl sts and the purl sts reverse to knit sts. 2) All the k1-wy3 sts are counted as 1 st when counting sts on the following row. When the k1-wy3 is worked as kw-f/b on the following row, the st count is increased by 1.

Row 1: K2, *k2tog-tbl, [k1-wy3] twice, k2tog, k3; repeat from * to last 8 sts, k2tog-tbl, [k1-wy3] twice, k2tog, k2.
Row 2: P3, *[kw-f/b] twice, p5; repeat from * to last 5 sts, [kw-f/b] twice, p3.
Row 3: K1, *k2tog-tbl, k1-wy3, p2, k1-wy3, k2tog, k1; repeat from * to end.
Row 4: P2, *kw-f/b, k2, kw-f/b, p3; repeat from * to last 6 sts, kw-f/b, k2, kw-f/b, p2.
Row 5: K2tog-tbl, *k1-wy3, p4, k1-wy3, sk2p; repeat from * to last 8 sts, k1-wy3, p4, k1-wy3, k2tog.
Row 6: P1, *kw-f/b, k4, kw-f/b, p1; repeat from * to end.
Row 7: Purl.
Repeat Rows 1-7 for Hills and Valleys.

A SIDE B SIDE

24 ANOTHER LACY RIB

Simple little patterns with small stitch multiples are often the staple of a knitter's cache of stitches. Here's an easy one to add to the group.

STITCH AND ROW INFORMATION

Multiple of 4 sts + 1; 6-row repeat.

NOTE

When knitting or purling a yo from a previous row, work it so that you create a hole (see Open the Yarnover, page 189).

Rows 1, 3, and 5 (A): P2, k1, *p3, k1; repeat from * to last 2 sts, p2.
Rows 2 and 4: K2tog, yo, p1, *yo, sk2p, yo, p1; repeat from * to last 2 sts, yo, skp.
Row 6: K2, p1, *k3, p1; repeat from * to last 2 sts, k2.
Repeat Rows 1-6 for Another Lacy Rib.

25 HALF NELSON

This stitch was inspired by the Marshmallow Sofa, a product of the George Nelson studio in the 1950s. It was actually designed by his associate Irving Harper, thus Nelson only gets half the credit. Wrestling aficionados may see another visual connection.

STITCH AND ROW INFORMATION
Multiple of 6 sts; 2-row repeat.

NOTE
The reverse side of this st pattern is a mirror image of the side shown.

Row 1: *[K1, p1] twice, k1, turn; [p1, k1] twice, p1, turn; [k1, p1] 3 times; repeat from * to end.
Row 2: *[K1, p1] 3 times, p5so, turn; k1, turn; holding working needle in left hand, KCO 5 sts to left-hand needle, [k1, p1] 3 times across these sts; repeat from * to end.
Repeat Rows 1 and 2 for Half Nelson, ending with Row 1.
BO Row: [K1, p1] 3 times, p5so, *yoc4, [k1, p1] 3 times, p6so; repeat from * to end. Cut yarn and pull through last st to fasten off.

26 DROPPED STITCHES

Often stitches are dropped intentionally and allowed to unravel down the length of one's knitting to create a lacy feel. For this pattern, stitches are dropped, but only allowed to run down several rows, resulting in an interesting, less lacy, woven-looking fabric.

STITCH AND ROW INFORMATION
Multiple of 9 sts + 6; 20-row repeat.

NOTE
When knitting or purling a yo from a previous row, work it so that you close the hole (see Close the Yarnover, page 189).

Row 1 (A): *P6, k3; repeat from * to last 6 sts, p6.
Row 2: K4, *k2tog, p3, k1, yo, k3; repeat from * to last 2 sts, k2.
Row 3: P7, *k3, p6; repeat from * to last 8 sts, k3, p5.
Row 4: K3, *k2tog, p3, k1, yo, k3; repeat from * to last 3 sts, k3.
Row 5: P8, *k3, p6; repeat from * to last 7 sts, k3, p4.
Row 6: K2, *k2tog, p3, k1, yo, k3; repeat from * to last 4 sts, k4.
Row 7: P9, *k3, p6; repeat from * to last 6 sts, k3, p3.
Row 8: K1, *k2tog, p3, k1, yo, k3; repeat from * to last 5 sts, k5.
Row 9: P10, *k3, p6; repeat from * to last 5 sts, k3, p2.
Row 10: K2, *p3, k4, drop 1, yo, k1; repeat from * to last 4 sts, k4. Unravel dropped st back to Row 2.
Row 11: Repeat Row 1.
Row 12: K5, *yo, k1, p3, skp, k3; repeat from * to last st, k1.
Row 13: P5, *k3, p6; repeat from * to last st, p1.
Row 14: K6, *yo, k1, p3, skp, k3; repeat from * to end.
Row 15: P4, *k3, p6; repeat from * to last 2 sts, p2.
Row 16: K7, *yo, k1, p3, skp, k3; repeat from * to last 8 sts, yo, k1, p3, skp, k2.
Row 17: P3, *k3, p6; repeat from * to last 3 sts, p3.
Row 18: K8, *yo, k1, p3, skp, k3; repeat from * to last 7 sts, yo, k1, p3, skp, k1.
Row 19: P2, *k3, p6; repeat from * to last 4 sts, p4.
Row 20: K5, *drop 1, yo, k4, p3, k1; repeat from * to last st, k1. Unravel dropped st back to Row 12.
Repeat Rows 1-20 for Dropped Stitches.

A SIDE

B SIDE

27 NOYO BOXES

Noyo stands for no yarnovers. The swatch shown here is in its natural state, but could be blocked like traditional lace to create more open space. I like the way the boxes curl toward the knit side, the way Stockinette stitch is inclined to do, so I chose not to stretch or flatten the sample.

STITCH AND ROW INFORMATION
Multiple of 9 sts; 5-row repeat.

NOTE

On the opposite side of the swatch shown, the knit sts reverse to purl sts and the purl sts reverse to knit sts.

CO a minimum of 18 sts.
Rows 1 and 3: Slip 1 knitwise, k2, *p6, k3; repeat from * to last 6 sts, p6.
Rows 2 and 4: Slip 1 knitwise, k5, *p3, k6; repeat from * to last 3 sts, p3.
Row 5: Slip 1 knitwise, k2, pso, AO-h 4 sts, *p1, [p1, pso] 5 times, AO-h 2 sts, k1, [k1, pso] twice, AO-h 5 sts; repeat from * to last 6 sts, p1, [p1, pso] 4 times, AO-h 1 st, p1.
Repeat Rows 1-5 for Noyo Boxes, ending final repeat with Row 4.
BO Row: Working Row 1, BO all sts in pattern.

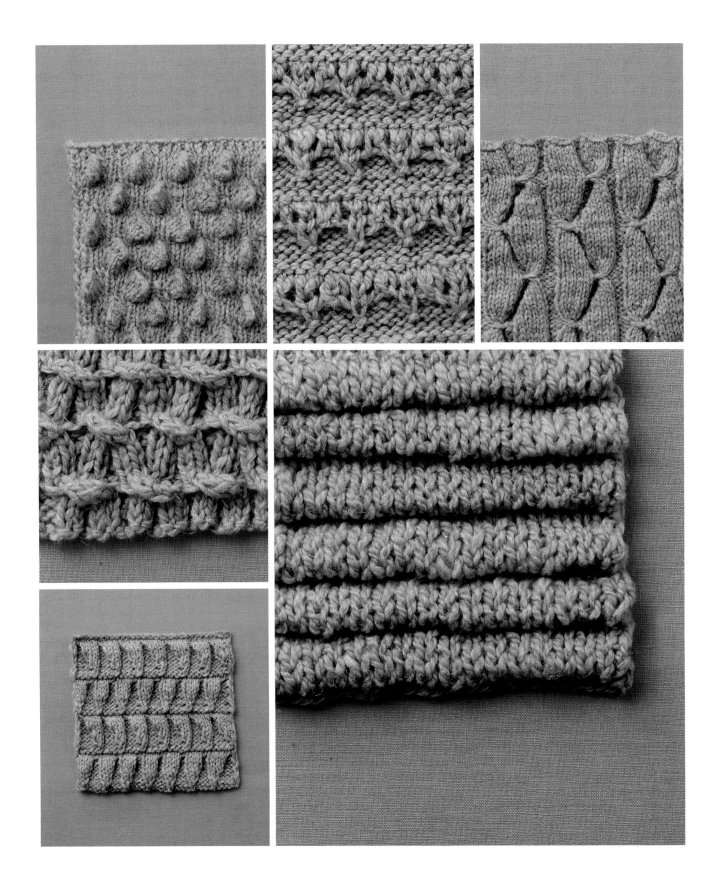

DIVIDE & COMBINE

When stitches are divided onto two separate needles, it becomes possible to work two sides of a knit fabric separately and, therefore, differently (see Divide Stitches, page 185, and Combine Stitches, page 179). It also allows a third dimension to rise from the fabric. Afterward, combining the stitches completes the intended effect and locks the shape into position.

The way I apply the concepts of divide and combine may look different from other stitch patterns, but if you have ever made a knit cable, you may recognize an operational similarity. Some stitches are separated from the rest, manipulated, and then reunited with the others once again.

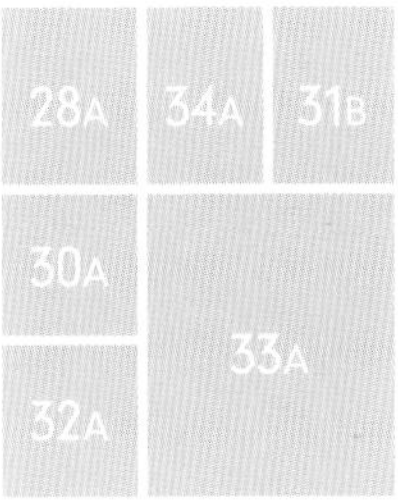

28A	34A	31B
30A	33A	
32A		

28A Fins
30A I-Cord Cables
31B Cut Cables
32A Blocks and Triangles
33A Puffy
34A Embossed

28 FINS

I enjoy the visual contradiction between this stitch pattern's spiky forms and the softness of the yarn in which I worked it. I'm considering using this pattern to make a wide bracelet in a shiny bamboo or silk metallic-color yarn.

A SIDE

B SIDE

STITCH AND ROW INFORMATION

Multiple of 10 sts + 11 at CO (st count varies through pattern); 12-row repeat.

NOTES

1) Requires 2 double-pointed needles (dpn) the same size as working needles. 2) Create a yo using the Alternative method (see Alternative Yarnover, page 188). 3) When knitting or purling a yo from a previous row, work it so that you close the hole (see Close the Yarnover, page 189).

ABBREVIATION

MF (Make Fin): Slip next 4 sts to first dpn, slip next 3 sts to second dpn, fold second dpn behind and parallel to first dpn; with working needle, [k1 from front dpn, p1 from back dpn] 3 times, k1 from front dpn until 7 sts have been combined (see Combine Stitches, page 179), turn; with empty dpn, BO 6 sts in rib pattern, slip last st purlwise wyif back to left-hand needle, turn.

Row 1 (B): Slip 1 knitwise, p1, k1, p5, *[k1, p1] twice, k1, p5; repeat from * to last 3 sts, k1, p1, k1.

Row 2: Slip 1 purlwise, k1, p1, yo, k5, yo, *[p1, k1] twice, p1, yo, k5, yo; repeat from * to last 3 sts, p1, k1, p1.

Row 3: Slip 1 knitwise, p1, k1, p7, *[k1, p1] twice, k1, p7; repeat from * to last 3 sts, k1, p1, k1.

Row 4: Slip 1 purlwise, k1, p1, yo, k7, yo, *[p1, k1] twice, p1, yo, k7, yo; repeat from * to last 3 sts, p1, k1, p1.

Row 5: Slip 1 knitwise, p1, k1, p9, *[k1, p1] twice, k1, p9; repeat from * to last 3 sts, k1, p1, k1.

Row 6: Slip 1 purlwise, k1, p1, k1, MF, *k1, p1, yo, k3, yo, p1, k1, MF; repeat from * to last 4 sts, [k1, p1] twice.

Row 7: Slip 1 knitwise, [p1, k1] 3 times, *p5, [k1, p1] twice, k1; repeat from * to last 2 sts, p1, k1.

Row 8: Slip 1 purlwise, [k1, p1] 3 times, *yo, k5, yo, [p1, k1] twice, p1; repeat from * to last 2 sts, k1, p1.

Row 9: Slip 1 knitwise, [p1, k1] 3 times, *p7, [k1, p1] twice, k1; repeat from * to last 2 sts, p1, k1.

Row 10: Slip 1 purlwise, [k1, p1] 3 times, *yo, k7, yo, [p1, k1] twice, p1; repeat from * to last 2 sts, k1, p1.

Row 11: Slip 1 knitwise, [p1, k1] 3 times, *p9, [k1, p1] twice, k1; repeat from * to last 2 sts, p1, k1.

Row 12: Slip 1 purlwise, k1, p1, *yo, k3, yo, p1, k1, MF, k1, p1; repeat from * to last 6 sts, yo, k3, yo, p1, k1, p1.

Repeat Rows 1-12 for Fins.

| A SIDE | B SIDE |

29 BANDS AND FOLDS

This stitch pattern has a subtler three-dimensional feel than others in this category. Its knit 1, purl 1 foundation makes it easy to mix together with a simple rib.

STITCH AND ROW INFORMATION
Multiple of 12 sts + 4; 8-row repeat.

NOTES
1) Requires 2 sets of needles 3 sizes apart and 1 double-pointed needle (dpn) the same size as smaller needles. 2) When using a larger needle to work sts from a smaller needle, insert only the tapered tip of the larger needle into the st to be worked. The size of the new st is determined by the size of the right-hand needle after the st has been worked.

CO sts with smaller needle.

Row 1 (B): Slip 1 knitwise, p1, *k1, p1; repeat from * to end.

Rows 2 and 3: Repeat Row 1.

Rows 4 and 6: Change to larger needle. Slip 1 knitwise, p1, knit to last st, p1.

Rows 5 and 7: Slip 1 knitwise, purl to last 2 sts, k1, p1.

Row 8: Change to smaller needle. Slip 1 knitwise, p1, *slip next 6 sts to dpn and hold in front of next 6 sts, [k1 from dpn, p1 from back needle] 6 times; repeat from * to last 2 sts, k1, p1.

Repeat Rows 1-8 for Bands and Folds.

30 I-CORD CABLES

I like taking something that is peripheral, usually playing a supporting role, and placing it front and center as the lead, thus my desire to create an I-Cord stitch pattern. You'll find a second one as well (see Cabled Rib Cord, page 36).

STITCH AND ROW INFORMATION
Multiple of 8 sts + 2; 12-row repeat.

NOTES
1) Requires 2 additional circular (circ) or double-pointed needles (dpn) and 1 cable needle (cn) the same size as working needles.
2) When slipping sts on Rows 5 and 11, make sure yarn remains to back and does not get caught between slipped sts.

Rows 1 and 3 (A): K2, *p2, k2; repeat from * to end.
Rows 2 and 4: P2, *k2, p2; repeat from * to end. Divide sts onto 2 circ needles or dpns (see Divide Stitches, page 185), as follows: With A side facing, slip all knit sts to front needle and all purl sts to back needle. *Note: There will be 2 more sts on front needle than on back.*
Row 5: Working on front needle only, *k2, [slip these 2 sts back to left-hand needle, k2] 4 times, slip 2 sts from right-hand needle to cn, hold to front, slip 2 sts from next needle to right-hand needle, slip 2 sts from cn to right-hand needle; repeat from * to last 2 sts, k2, turn. *Note: Back needle is not worked on Row 5.*
Row 6: Work both needles to recombine sts (see Combine Stitches, page 179), as follows: With B side facing you, using empty needle, p2 from back needle, *k2 from front needle, p2 from back needle; repeat from * to end.
Rows 7 and 9: Repeat Row 1.
Rows 8 and 10: Repeat Row 2. Divide sts onto 2 circ needles or dpns, as follows: With A side facing, slip all knit sts to front needle and all purl sts to back needle. *Note: There will be 2 more sts on front needle than on back.*
Row 11: Working on front needle only, k2, *k2, [slip last 2 sts back to left-hand needle, k2] 4 times, slip 2 sts from right-hand needle to cn, hold to front, slip 2 sts from next needle to right-hand needle, slip 2 sts from cn to right-hand needle; repeat from * to end, turn. *Note: Back needle is not worked on Row 11.*
Row 12: Work both needles to recombine sts, as follows: With B side facing, using empty needle, *p2 from back needle, slip 2 from front needle to cn, hold to front, k2 from front needle, p2 from back needle, k2 from cn; repeat from * to last 2 sts, p2 from back needle.
Repeat Rows 1-12 for I-Cord Cables.

A SIDE

B SIDE

31 CUT CABLES

With its two very different-looking sides, Cut Cables appears
difficult to knit, though it really isn't. To create a scarf for a friend,
I worked it in a three-pattern repeat in Rowan Felted Tweed.

| A SIDE | B SIDE |

STITCH AND ROW INFORMATION
Multiple of 18 sts + 3; 20-row repeat.

NOTE
Requires 2 double-pointed needles (dpn) the same size as working needles.

Rows 1, 3, and 5 (A): K3, *p5, k5, p5, k3; repeat from * to end.
Rows 2, 4, and 6: P3, *k5, p5, k5, p3; repeat from * to end.
Row 7: K3, *slip next 5 sts to first dpn, slip next 5 sts to second dpn, fold second dpn behind and parallel to first dpn; with working needle, [p1 from back dpn, p1 from front dpn] 5 times until 10 sts have been combined (see Combine Stitches, page 179), turn; with dpn, BO 4 of the combined sts knitwise; hold empty dpn in front of dpn with 1 st, slip 1 st from previous needle to front dpn, then 1 st to back dpn until there are 3 sts on each dpn; slip 3 sts on back dpn to previous needle, turn; knit 3 sts on remaining dpn onto previous needle, do not turn; from next needle p5, k3; repeat from * to end.
Row 8: P3, *k5, p1, p1-b/f, p1, k1, k1-b/f, k1, p3; repeat from * to end.

Row 9: K3, *p4, k4, p5, k3; repeat from * to end.
Row 10: P3, *k5, p2, p1-b/f, p1, k1, k1-b/f, k2, p3; repeat from * to end.
Rows 11, 13, and 15: K3, *p5, k5, p5, k3; repeat from * to end.
Rows 12, 14, and 16: P3, *k5, p5, k5, p3; repeat from * to end.
Row 17: K3, *p5, slip next 5 sts to first dpn, slip next 5 sts to second dpn, fold second dpn behind and parallel to first dpn, and with working needle, [k1 from front dpn, k1 from back dpn] 5 times until 10 sts have been combined, turn; with dpn, BO 4 of the combined sts purlwise; hold empty dpn in front of working dpn with 1 st, slip 1 st from previous needle to front dpn, then 1 st to back dpn until there are 3 sts on each dpn; slip 3 sts on front dpn to next needle and slip 3 sts from back dpn to previous needle so attached yarn is hanging from last st on previous needle, from next needle p3, k3; repeat from * to end.
Row 18: P3, *k1, k1-b/f, k1, p1, p1-b/f, p1, k5, p3; repeat from * to end.
Row 19: K3, *p5, k4, p4, k3; repeat from * to end.
Row 20: P3, *k1, k1-b/f, k2, p2, p1-b/f, p1, k5, p3; repeat from * to end.
Repeat Rows 1-20 for Cut Cables.

32 BLOCKS AND TRIANGLES

This deeply textured stitch pattern creates a nicely insulating fabric. The triangular shapes on side A are formed from increases; they are then knit together with the original stitches to create a secondary layer. Worked in a bulkier yarn than the DK-weight shown here, it would make a fabulously warm scarf for a cold winter.

A SIDE   B SIDE

Multiple of 5 sts + 2 (st count varies through pattern);
20-row repeat.

NOTES

1) Requires 1 additional double-pointed needle (dpn) no larger than working needles. 2) When knitting or purling a yo from a previous row, work it so that you close the hole (see Close the Yarnover, page 189).

Row 1 (A): Slip 1 knitwise, *p4, k1; repeat from * to last st, p1.
Row 2: Slip 1 knitwise, *p1, yo, k4; repeat from * to last st, p1.
Row 3: Slip 1 knitwise, *p4, k2; repeat from * to last st, p1.
Row 4: Slip 1 knitwise, *p2, yo, k4; repeat from * to last st, p1.
Row 5: Slip 1 knitwise, *p4, k3; repeat from * to last st, p1.
Row 6: Slip 1 knitwise, *p3, yo, k4; repeat from * to last st, p1.
Rows 7 and 8: Slip 1 knitwise, *p4, k4; repeat from * to last st, p1.
Row 9: Slip 1 knitwise, *slip next 4 sts to dpn, hold to back, [k2tog (1 st from next needle together with 1 st from dpn)] 4 times; repeat from * to last st, k1.
Row 10: Slip 1 purlwise, *k4, yo; repeat from * to last st, k1.
Row 11: Slip 1 purlwise, *k1, p4; repeat from * to last st, k1.

Row 12: Slip 1 purlwise, *k4, yo, p1; repeat from * to last st, k1.
Row 13: Slip 1 purlwise, *k2, p4; repeat from * to last st, k1.
Row 14: Slip 1 purlwise, *k4, yo, p2; repeat from * to last st, k1.
Row 15: Slip 1 purlwise, *k3, p4; repeat from * to last st, k1.
Row 16: Slip 1 purlwise, *k4, yo, p3; repeat from * to last st, k1.
Rows 17 and 18: Slip 1 purlwise, *k4, p4; repeat from * to last st, k1.
Row 19: Slip 1 purlwise, *slip next 4 sts to dpn, hold to front, [k2tog (1 st from dpn together with 1 st from next needle)] 4 times; repeat from * to last st, k1.
Row 20: Slip 1 purlwise, *yo, k4; repeat from * to last st, p1.
Repeat Rows 1-20 for Blocks and Triangles, ending final repeat with Row 9 or 19.
BO Row: BO all sts knitwise.

33 PUFFY

While I'm not exactly a fan of the puffy jackets that first became popular in the 1980s, I love taking something that doesn't naturally interest me, and turning it into something I find appealing. I think this stitch, used judiciously, could give puffy a good name.

STITCH AND ROW INFORMATION

Odd number of sts; 10-row repeat.

NOTE

Requires 2 additional circular (circ) or double-pointed needles (dpn) the same size as working needles.

Rows 1 and 3 (B): Slip 1 purlwise, *k1, p1; repeat from * to end.

Row 2: Slip 1 knitwise, *p1, k1; repeat from * to end.

Divide sts onto 2 circ needles or dpns (see Divide Stitches, page 185), as follows: With A side facing, slip all knit sts (Puffy sts) to front needle, and all purl sts to back needle. *Note: There will be 1 more st on front needle than on back.*

Note: Work Rows 4-9 on Puffy sts only.

Row 4: Working on Puffy sts only, *k1, yo; repeat from * to last st, k1.

Rows 5 and 7: Slip 1 purlwise, purl to end.

Rows 6 and 8: Slip 1 knitwise, knit to end.

Row 9: *P1, drop 1 st, repeat from * to last st, p1. Unravel dropped sts back to Row 4.

Row 10: Work both needles to combine sts (see Combine Stitches, page 179), as follows: With A side facing, using working needle, k1 from front needle, *p1 from back needle, k1 from front needle; repeat from * to end.

Repeat Rows 1-10 for Puffy.

34 EMBOSSED

If you knit a sample of this stitch pattern to understand the concept, you'll see that you can readily adapt it to create your own embossed designs. To create the embossed overlay, increases are made on Row 2 and then slipped onto a separate needle from the original stitches. Both needles are worked in the round to keep the original stitches growing in length at the same rate as the embossed pattern. When the pattern on the embossed side is complete, the stitches from both needles are knit together.

STITCH AND ROW INFORMATION

Multiple of 4 sts + 2 (st count varies through pattern); 8-row repeat.

NOTE

Requires 2 additional circular (circ) or double-pointed needles (dpn) the same size as working needles.

Row 1 (A): Purl.
Row 2: *K1-f/b, k3; repeat from * to last 2 sts, k1-f/b, k1.
Divide sts onto 2 circ needles or dpns (see Divide Stitches, page 185), as follows: With A side facing, slip 1 st to back needle, slip 1 st to front needle, *slip 4 sts to back needle, slip 1 st to front needle; repeat from * to last st, slip 1 st to back needle. *Note: Increases from Row 2 have been slipped to front needle (Embossed Needle) and all other sts have been slipped to back needle (Main Needle).*
Note: Rnds 3-6 are worked in the round on 2 needles.
Rnd 3: Embossed Needle: *K1, yo; repeat from * to last st on needle, k1; Main Needle: Knit.
Rnd 4: Embossed Needle: *K1, k1-b/f in yo; repeat from * to last st on needle, k1; Main Needle: Knit.
Rnd 5: Embossed Needle: K1, *yo, k1, yo, k2tog; repeat from * to end of needle; Main Needle: Knit.
Rnd 6: Both Needles: Knit. *Note: Work all yo's from Row 5 so that you create a hole (see Open the Yarnover, page 189).*
Row 7: *Note: Embossed Needle is not worked on this row.* Main Needle: Purl.
Row 8: Work both needles to combine sts (see Combine Sitches, page 179), as follows: With Main Needle in front, *k2tog (1 st from Main Needle together with 1 st from Embossed Needle); repeat from * to last st, k1 from Main Needle.
Repeat Rows 1-8 for Embossed.

A SIDE

B SIDE

35 TUCKS AND CABLES

Starting with a rib pattern, then dividing it onto two
needles, is an easy way to create knit fabric with a different
look on each side. For this stitch, side B is simply left
on hold while the tucks on side A are created. Then when
the two sides are reunited, the stitches on side B are
crossed to form the cables.

| A SIDE | B SIDE |

STITCH AND ROW INFORMATION

Multiple of 12 sts + 3 (st count varies through pattern);
24-row repeat.

NOTES

1) Requires 2 additional circular (circ) or double-pointed needles (dpn) the same size as working needles. 2) Hide all wraps as you come to them.

CO at least 27 sts.

Rows 1, 3, and 5 (A): K3, *p3, k3; repeat from * to end.

Rows 2, 4, and 6: P3, *k3, p3; repeat from * to end.

Divide stitches onto 2 circ needles or dpns (see Divide Stitches, page 185), as follows: With A side facing, slip all knit sts (Tuck sts) to front needle and all purl sts (Cable sts) to back needle. *Note: There will be 3 more sts on front needle than on back.* *Note: Work Rows 7-9 on Tuck sts only.*

Row 7: Working on Tuck sts only, *k5, w&t; p4, w&t; k3, w&t; p2, w&t; k4, yo; repeat from * to last 3 sts, k3.

Row 8: Purl.

Row 9: *K5, k2tog; repeat from * to last 3 sts, k3.

Row 10: Work both needles to combine sts (see Combine Stitches, page 179), as follows: With B side facing, using working needle, *p3 from back needle, slip 3 sts from front needle to cn, hold behind front needle, k3 from front needle, p3 from back needle, k3 from cn; repeat from * to last 3 sts, p3 from back needle.

Rows 11, 13, 15, and 17: K3, *p3, k3; repeat from * to end.

Rows 12, 14, 16, and 18: P3, *k3, p3; repeat from * to end.

Divide stitches onto 2 circ needles or dpns, as follows: With A side facing, slip all knit sts to front needle and all purl sts to back needle. *Note: There will be 3 more sts on front needle than on back.* *Note: Work Rows 19-21 on Tuck sts only.*

Row 19: Working on Tuck sts only, k3, *yo, k5, w&t; p4, w&t; k3, w&t; p2, w&t; k4; repeat from * to end.

Row 20: Purl.

Row 21: *K2, k2tog, *k5, k2tog; repeat from * to last 6 sts, k6.

Row 22: Work both needles to combine sts, as follows: With B side facing, using working needle, p3 from back needle, k3 from front needle, *p3 from back needle, slip 3 sts from front needle to cn, hold to front, k3 from front needle, p3 from back needle, k3 from cn; repeat from * to last 9 sts, p3 from back needle, k3 from front needle, p3 from back needle.

Row 23: Repeat Row 1.

Row 24: Repeat Row 2.

Repeat Rows 1-24 for Tucks and Cables, ending with Row 4.

BO all sts in pattern.

36 FOUR-BY-FOUR SHIFT

This is my interpretation of a broken rib stitch, which can easily be adapted from a knit 4, purl 4 into different rib multiples, such as knit 2, purl 2, or knit 3, purl 3. When I worked this stitch pattern in the smaller rib variations, I still maintained the four even rows of rib worked in Rows 1-4 and 8-11, but you could alter that as well.

STITCH AND ROW INFORMATION

Multiple of 8 sts (st count varies through pattern); 14-row repeat.

NOTES

1) This stitch pattern looks identical on both sides.
2) Requires 1 additional double-pointed needle (dpn) no larger than working needles.

Rows 1-4: *K4, p4; repeat from * to end.
Row 5: *[K1-wy3] 4 times, [p1-wy3] 4 times; repeat from * to end.
Row 6: *[Kw-f/b] 4 times, [pw-f/b] 4 times; repeat from * to end (you should have twice the number of sts you CO).
Row 7: *Slip 8 sts to dpn, hold to front, [p2tog (1 st from next needle together with 1 st from dpn)] 4 times, [k2tog (1 st from next needle together with 1 st from dpn)] 4 times, repeat from * to end.
Rows 8-11: *P4, k4; repeat from * to end.
Row 12: *[P1-wy3] 4 times, [k1-wy3] 4 times; repeat from * to end.
Row 13: *[Pw-f/b] 4 times, [kw-f/b] 4 times; repeat from * to end (you should have twice the number of sts you CO).
Row 14: *Slip 8 sts to dpn, hold to back, [k2tog (1 st from next needle together with 1 st from dpn)] 4 times, [p2tog (1 st from next needle together with 1 st from dpn)] 4 times; repeat from * to end.
Repeat Rows 1-14 for Four-by-Four Shift.

REVERSIBLE STITCH PATTERNS

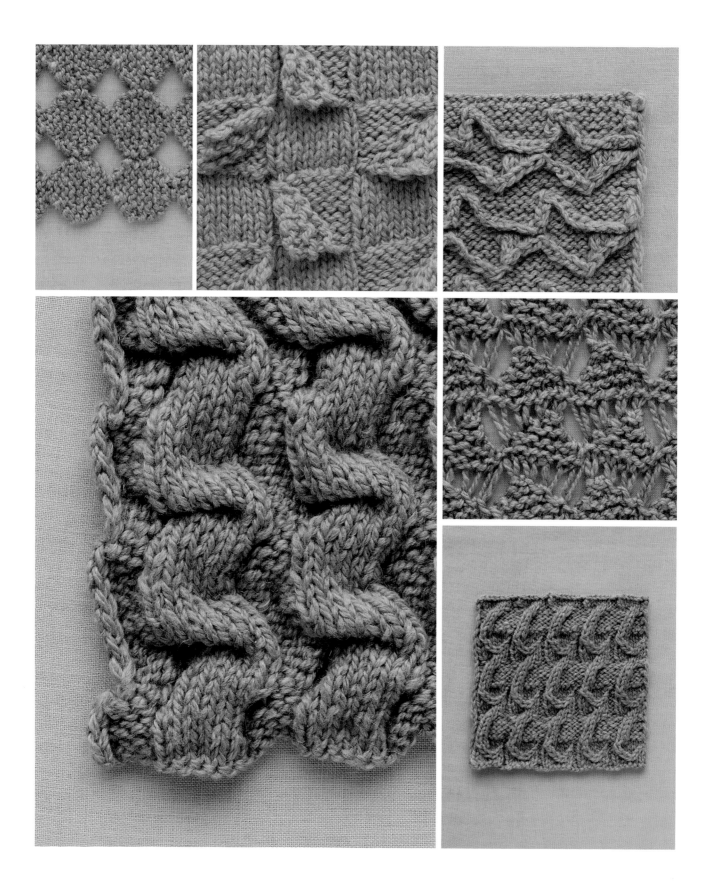

PICKED UP

In most traditional knitting, stitches are usually picked up for a functional use–to add a button band to a cardigan, finish the neck of a sweater, or begin the gusset of a sock. But for this set of stitches, I chose to use pick-ups in a purely decorative way, taking advantage of their versatility, since stitches can be picked up from anywhere in your knitting, and may even be worked to distant places across the fabric. In Folded Fabric (#43) the pick-ups are made seven rows down from the attached yarn, while in Pick-Up Overlay (#38) the pick-ups, combined with yarnover chains (see page 189), allow the working yarn to "draw" its way across the width of the finished knitting to the opposite side.

37 CHECKS AND FLAPS

Essentially, this is a checkerboard Stockinette and Reverse Stockinette stitch pattern. The flaps are created by picking up stitches and working them onto finished squares. This gives you the freedom to design a checkerboard garment with flaps placed exactly where you want them, such as on cuffs or collars, for dramatic effect.

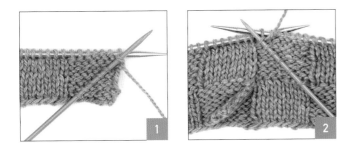

STITCH AND ROW INFORMATION

Multiple of 14 sts; 16-row repeat.

NOTES

1) Requires 2 double-pointed needles (dpn) the same size as working needles and 1 additional, smaller size dpn to pick up sts. 2) Do not hide wraps.

ABBREVIATION

MF (Make Flap): With smaller dpn, pick up 6 sts on the diagonal (see photo 1 for Row 7; see photo 2 for Row 15). Change to larger dpns for remainder of Flap. K6, turn; k5, w&t; k5, turn; k3, w&t; k3, turn; BO 5 sts, slip last st from dpn to right-hand needle.

Set-Up Row (B): *P7, k7; repeat from * to end.
Rows 1-6: *P7, k7; repeat from * to end.
Row 7: *MF, p7, k7; repeat from * to end.
Row 8: *K7, p6, p2tog; repeat from * to end.
Rows 9-14: *K7, p7; repeat from * to end.
Row 15: *K7, p7, MF; repeat from * to end.
Row 16: *P2tog, p6, k7; repeat from * to end.
Repeat Rows 1-16 for Checks and Flaps.

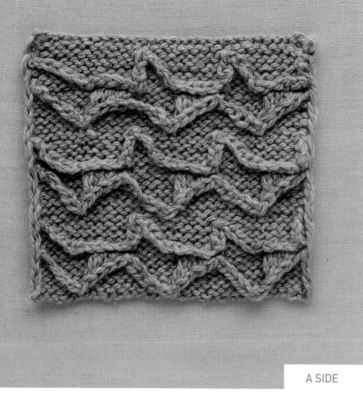

| A SIDE | B SIDE |

38 PICK-UP OVERLAY

Since overlays are worked on top of finished sections of Reverse Stockinette stitch, they can be placed nearly anywhere, allowing for easy shaping of the fabric. Overlay patterns also make fabulous embellishments worked in flattering places on an otherwise simple garment.

STITCH AND ROW INFORMATION

Multiple of 10 sts + 1; 12-row repeat.

NOTE

Requires 1 circular (circ) needle as working needle and 2 double-pointed needles (dpn) the same size as circ needle.

CO a minimum of 21 sts.

Set-Up Row (A): Purl.

Rows 1, 3, and 5: Slip 1 knitwise, knit to end.

Rows 2 and 4: Slip 1 purlwise, purl to end.

Note: Row 6 does not work any sts on the circ needle; all worked sts are picked up from sts in previous rows.

Row 6: Change to dpns. Skip first st, [pick up and purl 1 st from purl bump at base of next st on circ needle] 5 times (see photo 1). *Turn and work the 5 sts, as follows: Using second dpn, slip 1, k2, k2tog, turn; p2tog, p2, turn; slip 1, k2tog, turn; p2tog. Do not turn. Pick up and knit 1 st in seventh purl bump below next st on circ needle (see photos 2 and 3), pso, yoc5.** *Note: When working Row 6 for the first time, you will pick up this st from the CO row.*

Skip next 4 sts on circ needle, pick up and purl 1 st from purl bump at base of next st on circ needle (see photo 4), pso, [pick up and purl 1 st from purl bump at base of next st on circ needle] 4 times (see photo 5). Repeat from *, ending final repeat at **. Leave last st on dpn for Row 7.

Row 7: Hold dpn behind circ needle. Slip 1 knitwise from circ needle, k2tog (1 st from circ needle together with 1 st from dpn), knit to end.

Rows 8 and 10: Slip 1 purlwise, purl to end.

Row 9: Slip 1 knitwise, knit to end.

Note: Row 11 does not work any sts on the circ needle; all worked sts are picked up from sts in previous rows.

Row 11: Change to dpns. Turn work upside down so that circ needle is at bottom with purl side facing you. Skip first st, pick up and knit 1 st from purl bump at base of next st on circ needle (see photo 6).

*Yoc5, pick up and knit 1 st at right corner of triangle from Row 6 (see photos 7 and 8), pso, yoc4, pick up and knit 1 st at left corner of same triangle (see photos 9 and 10), pso, yoc3**; turn work right-side up so that circ needle is at top, with purl side facing; pick up and knit 1 st in purl bump at base of st on circ needle directly above last st picked up (see photo 11), pso. Turn work upside down. Repeat from *, ending final repeat at **. Leave last st on dpn for Row 12.

Row 12: Hold dpn in front of circ needle. Slip 1 purlwise from circ needle, p2tog (1 st from circ needle together with 1 st from dpn), purl to end.

Repeat Rows 1-12 for Pick-Up Overlay.

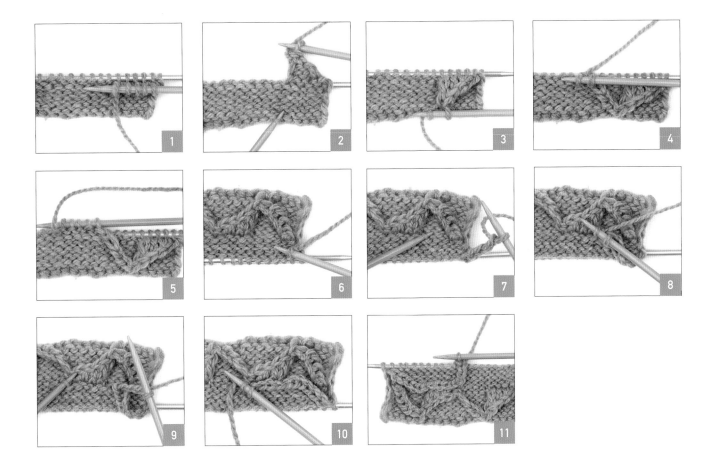

J CABLES

Occasionally during the development of this book, when I didn't have a clear vision of a stitch to work on, I would simply start manipulating rib variations. In this case, I began with a subtly cabled rib, then gave side A a different look by adding a picked-up curve.

| A SIDE | B SIDE |

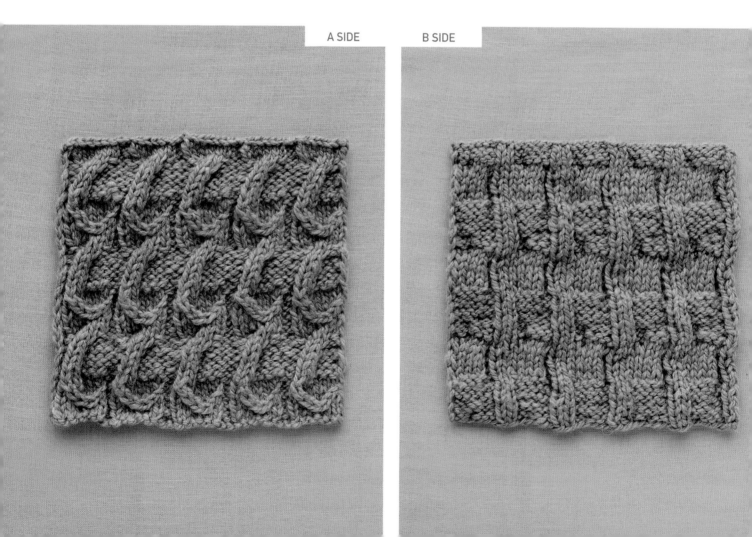

Multiple of 8 sts + 1; 14-row repeat.

NOTE

Requires 2 double-pointed needles (dpn) the same size as working needle, and 1 cable needle (cn) (optional; you may use a dpn in place of cn).

ABBREVIATION

KC (Knit Curve): Using dpns, following photo above, pick up and knit sts 1 and 2, pso (see Pick-Ups, page 185); pick up and knit remaining 4 sts in order indicated in photo, working pso after each picked-up st–1 st remains. Slip st to right-hand needle wyib.

CO a minimum of 17 sts.

Rows 1, 3, and 5 (A): K7, *p2, k6; repeat from * to last 2 sts, p2.

Rows 2, 4, and 6: *K2, p6; repeat from * to last st, p1.

Row 7: Slip 1, *slip 6 sts purlwise wyif, KC, p2; repeat from * to end.

Row 8: K2, *p2tog, p1, k6; repeat from * to last 8 sts, p2tog, p1, k5.

Rows 9 and 11: P5, *k2, p6; repeat from * to last 4 sts, k2, p2.

Rows 10 and 12: K2, *p2, k6; repeat from * to last 7 sts, p2, k5.

Row 13: P2, *slip 3 sts to cn, hold to back, k2, p3 from cn, p3; repeat from * to last 7 sts, slip 3 sts to cn, k2, p3 from cn, p2.

Row 14: *K2, p6; repeat from * to last 9 sts, k2, p7.

Repeat Rows 1-14 for J Cables.

40 DROP LOOP STEPS

The raised triangles of this stitch visually emulate the look of an embroidered satin stitch composed of collective parallel threads. Stitches are picked up on a diagonal, knit with multiple wraps to elongate them, and then overlaid on the background fabric.

| A SIDE | B SIDE |

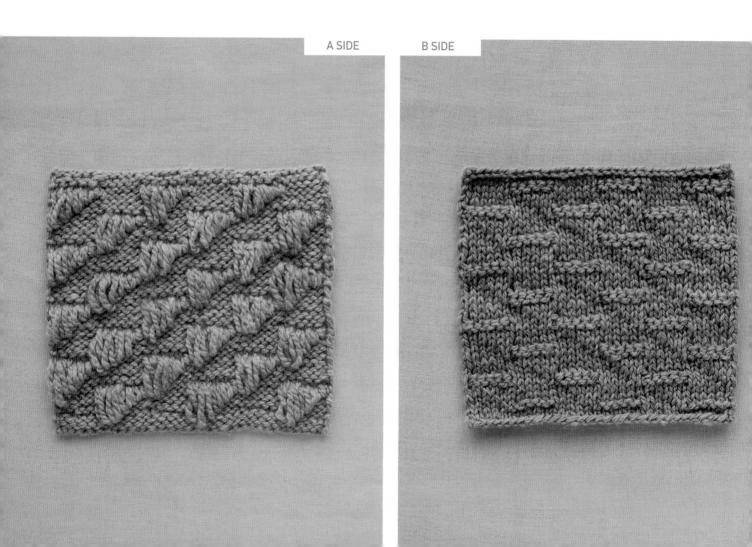

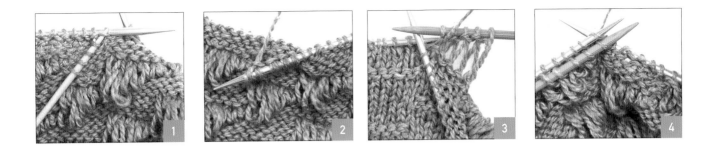

STITCH AND ROW INFORMATION

Multiple of 10 sts + 2; 8-row repeat.

NOTES

1) Requires 2 double-pointed needles (dpn), 1 the same size as working needles, and 1 at least 3 sizes smaller.

2) If pattern is worked with only 12 sts, do not work the sts between asterisks on Set-Up Row 3.

ABBREVIATION

MS (Make Step): Using smaller dpn, pick up 5 sts on the diagonal, beginning with second purl bump below next st on needle, and moving 1 st to the left and 1 row down for each of the next 4 sts (see photo 1). Using working needle, work the 5 picked-up sts as follows: K1, k1-wy2, k1-wy3, k1-wy4, k1-wy5 (see photo 2), turn. Change to larger dpn. P5, dropping extra wraps (see photo 3), turn. Hold dpn in front of next needle. Using previous needle, [k2tog (1 st from dpn together with 1 st from next needle, see photo 4)] 5 times.

Set-Up Row 1 (A): Purl.

Set-Up Row 2: Knit.

Set-Up Row 3: P6, *k5, p5; repeat from * to last 6 sts, k5, p1.

Rows 1 and 3: Knit.

Row 2: Purl.

Row 4: P1, *MS, p5; repeat from * to last st, p1.

Rows 5 and 7: Knit.

Row 6: Purl.

Row 8: P1, *p5, MS; repeat from * to last st, p1.

Repeat Rows 1-8 for Drop Loop Steps.

41 GARTER TRIANGLES

I worked several variations of these triangles before settling on this one, and you may have fun modifying them as well. This stitch pattern looks great as an allover fabric, or it can easily be inserted into a project as a decorative element.

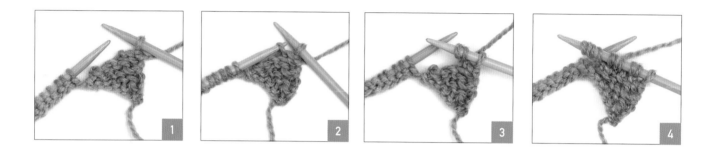

STITCH AND ROW INFORMATION
Multiple of 7 sts at CO (st count varies through pattern); 3-row repeat.

NOTE
The reverse side of this st pattern is a mirror image of the side shown.

ABBREVIATION
GT (Garter Triangle): K7, turn; k2tog, k3, k2tog, turn; k5, turn; k2tog, k1, k2tog, turn; k3, turn; k2tog, k1, turn; k2tog–1 st remains (see photo 1). Do not turn.
Pick up and k1-wy2 between first 2 purl ridges on left side of Triangle (see photos 2 and 3); pick up and k1-wy3 between next 2 ridges; pick up and k1-wy4 between last 2 ridges (see photo 4).

Row 1: Knit.
Row 2: *GT; repeat from * to end.
Row 3: *[Kw-f/b] 3 times; k1; repeat from * to end.
Repeat Rows 1-3 for Garter Triangles.

REVERSIBLE STITCH PATTERNS

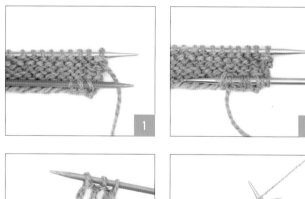

| A SIDE | B SIDE |

42 DROP LOOP CHECKS

The elongated stitches overlaid onto the background fabric here are worked similarly to Drop Loop Steps (page 70). These stitches are picked up horizontally, creating a very different look.

STITCH AND ROW INFORMATION
Multiple of 6 sts + 2; 12-row repeat.

NOTE
Requires 1 double-pointed needle (dpn), 1 size smaller than working needles.

ABBREVIATION
DL (Drop Loops): With dpn, pick up 3 sts in fifth purl row below next 3 sts on needle (see photo 1). Using working needle, work the 3 picked-up sts as follows: [K1-wy3] 3 times (see photo 2), turn; using dpn, p3, dropping extra wraps (see photo 3), turn. Hold dpn in front of next needle. Using previous needle, [k2tog (1 st from dpn together with 1 st from next needle, see photo 4)] 3 times.

Row 1 (B): K1, *p3, k3; repeat from * to last st, p1.
Rows 2 and 4: Purl.
Rows 3 and 5: Knit.
Row 6: K1, *DL, k3; repeat from * to last st, k1.
Row 7: P1, *k3, p3; repeat from * to last st, k1.
Rows 8 and 10: Purl.
Rows 9 and 11: Knit.
Row 12: K1, *k3, DL; repeat from * to last st, k1.
Repeat Rows 1-12 for Drop Loop Checks.

43 FOLDED FABRIC

This is an easy and adaptable stitch pattern. I worked it in the round for the Folded Mini Dress (page 118), and expanded it for the Folded Scarf (page 94).

STITCH AND ROW INFORMATION
Multiple of 12 sts; 9-row repeat.

NOTES
1) On the opposite side of the swatch shown, the knit sts reverse to purl sts and the purl sts reverse to knit sts.
2) Requires 1 double-pointed needle (dpn) 1 size smaller than working needles.

Rows 1-8: *K6, p6; repeat from * to end.
Row 9: *Rotate work forward so opposite side is showing and knitting is above needle. Using dpn, pick up sts 4-6 of current repeat on opposite side of work, 7 rows below current row (see photo 1). Rotate work back and hold dpn behind and parallel to main needle (see photo 2). [K2tog (1 st on main needle together with 1 st on dpn, see photo 2)] 3 times, k3, p6; repeat from * to end.
Repeat Rows 1-9 for Folded Fabric.

RUFFLED STRIPES

The raised ruffles on side A of Ruffled Stripes create a very different look than the plain Stockinette stitch on side B, while also adding a more feminine touch. Along with Pick-Up Overlay (page 66), this stitch pattern is an example of how different motifs can be embossed on Reverse Stockinette stitch.

A SIDE   B SIDE

STITCH AND ROW INFORMATION

Multiple of 6 sts at CO (st count varies through pattern);
16-row repeat.

NOTE

Requires 2 circular (circ) needles the same size as working needles.

CO a minimum of 12 sts.
Set-Up Row (A): Purl.
Row 1: Knit.
Row 2: Purl.
Row 3: K2, *k1-f/b, k5; repeat from * to last 4 sts, k1-f/b, k3. Turn.
Divide sts onto 2 circ needles (see Divide Stitches, page 185),
as follows: Slip 3 to back needle, *slip 1 to front needle, slip 6
to back needle; repeat from * to last 4 sts, slip 1 to front needle,
slip 3 to back needle. *Note: Increases from Row 3 have been
slipped to front needle (Increase Needle) and all other sts have
been slipped to back needle (Main Needle).*

Row 4: Working on Main Needle sts only, purl.
Row 5: *Note: Main Needle is not worked on this row.* With tip of
Increase Needle, pick up and knit 1 st in strand between first
and second sts on Main Needle, *yoc4 (see photo 1), knit next st
on Increase Needle (see photo 2), pso, yoc4**, with right-hand
needle pick up and knit 1 st in strand between sts on Main
Needle, halfway to next st on Increase Needle (see photo 3), pso
(see photo 4); repeat from *, ending final repeat at **. Leave last
st on needle. Turn.
Row 6: P2tog (last st from Increase Needle together with first
stitch from Main Needle), purl to end.
Rows 7-12: Repeat Rows 1-6.
Divide sts onto 2 circ needles, as follows: Slip 3 to back needle,
*slip 1 to front needle, slip 6 to back needle; repeat from * to last
3 sts, slip 3 to back needle.
Rows 13: Repeat Row 3.
Rows 14-16: Repeat Rows 4-6.
Repeat Rows 1-16 for Ruffled Stripes.

45 CIRCLES

This is a playful stitch pattern that would be fun to adapt to a wide array of projects, such as a multicolored set of placemats or as an alternative to ribbing on the bottom and cuffs of a sweater. Also, it would be easy to add circles to the ends of rows for a most unusual triangular shawl.

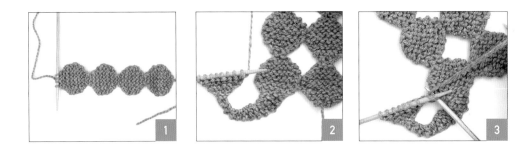

STITCH AND ROW INFORMATION

2 sts at CO (st count varies through pattern; circles can be added to increase width, columns of circles can be added to increase length).

NOTES

1) The reverse side of this st pattern is a mirror image of the side shown. 2) Short double-pointed needles (dpn) are easiest to work with given the small number of sts on the needle at any given time.

Set-Up Column: CO 2 sts, *[k1-f/b] twice, turn; [k1-f/b, knit to end, turn] 4 times; [k8, turn] 6 times; [k2tog, knit to end, turn] 4 times** ; [k2tog] twice, turn.
Repeat from * to desired number of circles in column, ending final repeat at ** (see photo 1).

Link Columns: [K4, turn] 4 times; k2, k2tog, turn; [k3, turn] 8 times; k1, k2tog, turn; [k2, turn] 8 times.
Next Column: *[K1-f/b] twice, turn; [k1-f/b, knit to end, turn] 4 times; [k8, turn] twice. Attach working circle to circle from previous column, as follows: Holding dpn with working yarn next to circle from previous column (see photo 2), wyib, pick up 1 edge st from circle from previous column, k2tog (picked up st together with first st on working needle, see photo 3), k7, turn; k8, turn; wyib, pick up 1 edge st from same circle, above first picked-up st, k2tog (picked up st together with first st on working needle), k7, turn; k8, turn; [k2tog, knit to end, turn] 4 times**; [k2tog] twice, turn.
Repeat from * for each circle from previous column, ending last circle of column at **.

Repeat Link Columns at end of each column to connect columns, then repeat Next Column. End final column at ** of Next Column, [k2tog] twice. On last repeat of final column, BO 2 sts knitwise.

DOUBLE KNIT

While I was working on this book, I saw a commercially made double-knit scarf with different patterns on each side. I had seen double knits where the two sides were the same pattern with colors inverted, but this was new to me. Both my curiosity about how it was made, and its relevance to the theme of the book, led me to devise a way to chart and knit them by hand. After I had designed several swatches, I noticed that most of them had the look of wallpaper from the 1950s! Unlike the stitches in the other sections, where each knitter can alter or use elements to create his or her own variations, the finished charts for these don't allow for such playfulness. However, I've included instructions on page 181 to help you create double knits of your own.

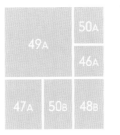

46A   Lattice Border and Checks
47A   Flipped Pair Border and Tweed
48B   Squares and Stripes
49A   Big Zag
50A   Half Moons and Bands
50B   Half Moons and Bands

46 LATTICE BORDER AND CHECKS

This stitch pattern is used for the yoke of the Double-Knit Vest (see page 110), where it provides the visual difference between the reversible sides. After the first ten rows, when the lattice and check section of the pattern is complete, the double knitting becomes simpler. This is because side A is now worked as a solid color. If you wish to work a fabric that is completely solid on side A from the beginning, work Rows 11-14 only.

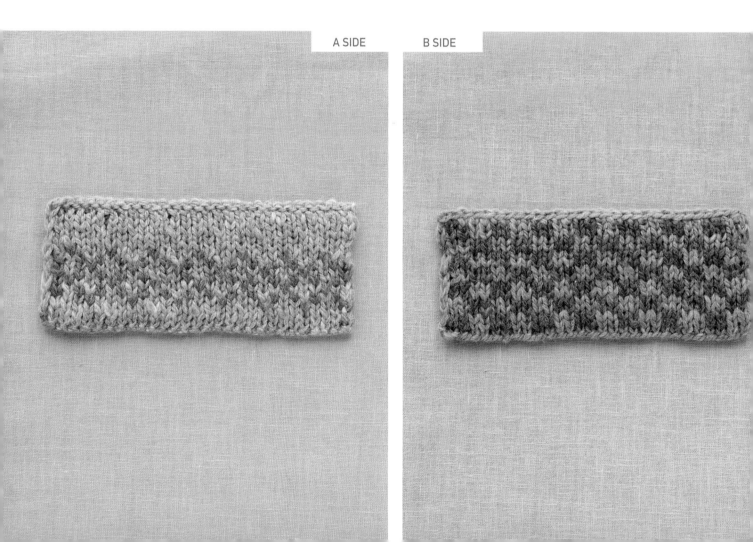

| A SIDE | B SIDE |

STITCH AND ROW INFORMATION

Multiple of 8 sts; 10-row pattern, A side lattice
border – B side checks.
Multiple of 8 sts; 4-row repeat, A side solid – B side checks.

Odd rows, A side facing:

Knit A side sts; purl B side sts.
Slip A side sts wyib; slip B side sts wyif.

Even rows, B side facing:

Purl A side sts; knit B side sts.
Slip A side sts wyif; slip B side sts wyib.

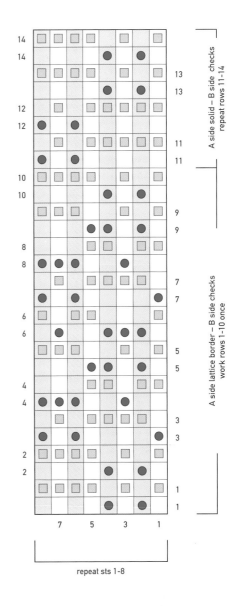

KEY

  A side – white columns

  B side – gray columns

  MC

CC

Slip all sts in empty squares purlwise.

47 FLIPPED PAIR BORDER AND TWEED

The flipped pair pattern shown here was my final choice from several possibilities. One placed the pairs closer together horizontally, and another shifted the "standing feet" pair up by one row to create a more undulating movement to the border. If you wish to eliminate the border design on side A for a completely solid-colored fabric while maintaining the tweed pattern on side B, only work Rows 13-14 of the chart. This could be a subtler alternate choice to the bold checks used in the Double-Knit Vest (see page 110).

STITCH AND ROW INFORMATION

Multiple of 32 sts; 12-row pattern, A side flipped pair border – B side tweed.
Multiple of 32 sts; 2-row repeat, A side solid – B side tweed.

Odd rows, A side facing:
Knit A side sts; purl B side sts.
Slip A side sts wyib; slip B side sts wyif.

Even rows, B side facing:
Purl A side sts; knit B side sts.
Slip A side sts wyif; slip B side sts wyib.

A SIDE	B SIDE

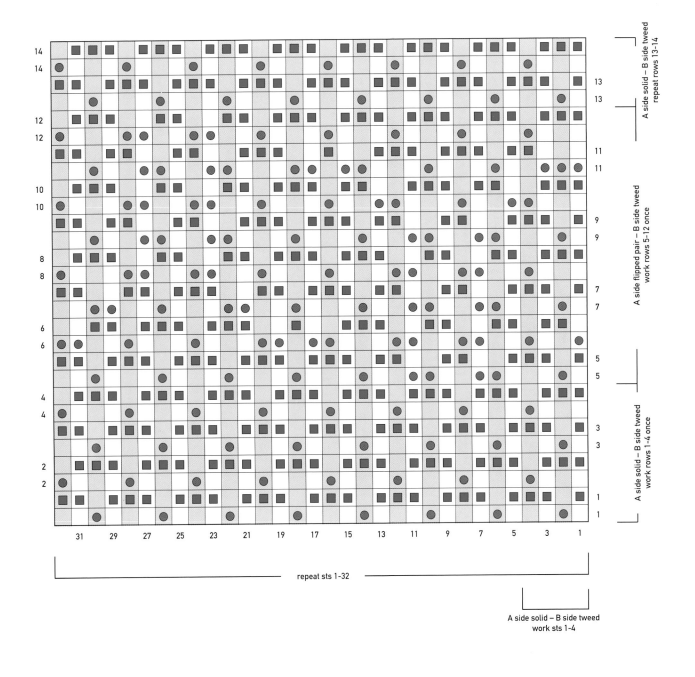

A side solid – B side tweed
repeat rows 13-14

A side flipped pair – B side tweed
work rows 5-12 once

A side solid – B side tweed
work rows 1-4 once

repeat sts 1-32

A side solid – B side tweed
work sts 1-4

KEY

A side – white columns

B side – gray columns

MC

CC

Slip all sts in empty squares purlwise.

A SIDE   B SIDE

48 SQUARES AND STRIPES

I think this combination of sporty stripes and classic squares would work nicely on a minimally shaped reversible jacket similar to Véronik Avery's Lice Jacket (see page 150). For an easier project, work the pattern as a scarf that will casually reveal both sides when nonchalantly wrapped around the neck.

STITCH AND ROW INFORMATION
Multiple of 48 sts; 30-row repeat.

Odd rows, A side facing:
Knit A side sts; purl B side sts.
Slip A side sts wyib; slip B side sts wyif.

Even rows, B side facing:
Purl A side sts; knit B side sts.
Slip A side sts wyif; slip B side sts wyib.

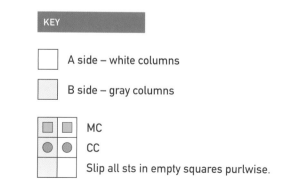

KEY

☐ A side – white columns

☐ B side – gray columns

MC

CC

Slip all sts in empty squares purlwise.

repeat rows 1-30

repeat sts 1-48

49 BIG ZAG

Double knitting couldn't be simpler than working this easy-to-memorize zigzag pattern opposite a solid-colored side. After the pattern is established, you may be able to work further repeats without reference to the chart.

A SIDE

B SIDE

STITCH AND ROW INFORMATION

Multiple of 8 sts; 16-row repeat.

Odd rows, A side facing:

Knit A side sts; purl B side sts.

Slip A side sts wyib; slip B side sts wyif.

Even rows, B side facing:

Purl A side sts; knit B side sts.

Slip A side sts wyif; slip B side sts wyib.

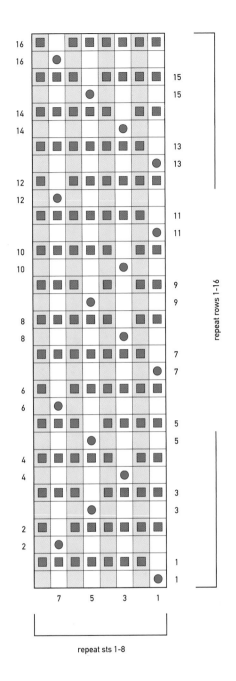

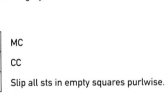

KEY

A side – white columns

B side – gray columns

MC

CC

Slip all sts in empty squares purlwise.

A SIDE   B SIDE

50 HALF MOONS AND BANDS

When working this pattern, you may find it helpful to place markers on your needles between repeats, just as lace knitters often do. It's much easier to check for errors across a small number of stitches within clearly marked repeats than across a long row. I also placed an additional marker between stitches 14 and 15 in the chart to indicate where the color change occurs between one vertical band and the next on side B.

STITCH AND ROW INFORMATION
Multiple of 28 sts; 26-row repeat.

Odd rows, A side facing:
Knit A side sts; purl B side sts.
Slip A side sts wyib; slip B side sts wyif.

Even rows, B side facing:
Purl A side sts; knit B side sts.
Slip A side sts wyif; slip B side sts wyib.

KEY	
☐	A side – white columns
☐	B side – gray columns

■	■	MC
○	○	CC

Slip all sts in empty squares purlwise.

repeat rows 1-26

repeat sts 1-28

REVERSIBLE
DESIGNS

folded scarf

LYNNE BARR

To create a generously sized scarf for a cold winter day, I expanded the Folded Fabric stitch (see page 75) from a twelve-stitch repeat up to a single twenty-six stitch pattern. Instead of using a single chunky yarn, I worked with two strands of lighter-weight yarn on larger needles, providing an almost imperceptible space between the yarns that allows a larger gauge while minimizing the density.

FINISHED MEASUREMENTS
7" wide x 68" long

YARN
Sheep Shop Yarn Company Sheep 3 (70% wool / 30% silk; 325 yards / 100 grams): 3 hanks #F101 Chartreuse

NEEDLES
One pair short straight needles size US 10½ (6.5 mm)
One double-pointed needle (dpn) size US 6 (4 mm) or smaller, to pick up stitches
Change needle size if necessary to obtain correct gauge.

GAUGE
13 sts = 4" (10 cm) in Stockinette stitch (St st), using larger needles and 2 strands of yarn held together

STITCH PATTERN
FOLDED FABRIC
(panel of 26 sts; 15-row repeat) *Note: This pattern is a variation of Folded Fabric on page 75; referenced photos show the method for creating folds in this scarf, but st numbers shown differ.*
Rows 1-14: Slip 1 st knitwise, k12, p13.
Row 15: Rotate work forward so opposite side is showing and knitting is above needle. Using dpn, pick up sts 7-13 of current repeat on opposite side of work, 13 rows below current row (see photo 1, page 75). Rotate work back and hold dpn behind and parallel to main needle (see photo 2, page 75). [K2tog (1 st from main needle together with 1 st from dpn)] 7 times, k6, p13.
Repeat Rows 1-15 for Folded Fabric. *Note: Because this pattern has a 15-row repeat, you will be working Row 15 on alternating sides of the piece.*

SCARF
Using larger needles and 2 strands of yarn held together, CO 26 sts; begin Folded Fabric. Work even until piece measures 68", or to desired length, ending with Row 8 of pattern. BO all sts in pattern.

branching ribs

LYNNE BARR

This boldly geometric scarf, which branches outward, retains a soft feminine shape when wrapped and layered like petals around your neck. Although it barely resembles the Folded Cables stitch that it was based on (see page 26), it is only a few changes away from its origin. The design went through three transformations (see page 5) before I was pleased with the version shown here.

FINISHED MEASUREMENTS

6" wide at widest point x 58" long

YARN

Blue Sky Alpacas Dyed Cotton (100% organically grown cotton; 150 yards / 100 grams): 3 hanks #605 Cumin

NEEDLES

One pair short straight needles size US 11 (8 mm)
Change needle size if necessary to obtain correct gauge.

GAUGE

16 sts = 4" (10 cm) in K1, P1 rib, using 2 strands of yarn held together, unstretched

SCARF

With 2 strands of yarn held together, CO 20 sts.

Notes: 1) Slip first st of every row knitwise. 2) When knitting or purling a yo from a previous row, work it so that you close the hole (see Close the Yarnover, page 189).

Rows 1-7: Slip 1, p1, *k1, p1; repeat from * to end.
Row 8: Slip 1, p1, [k1, p1] 4 times, yo, [k1, p1] 5 times–21 sts.
Row 9: *Slip 1, p1, [k1, p1] 4 times, w&t (wrap tightly); yo, [k1, p1] 5 times; repeat from * twice–24 sts.
Row 10: Slip 1, p1, [k1, p1] 4 times, w&t (wrap tightly);
yo, [k1, p1] 4 times, w&t; [k1, p1] 4 times, w&t (wrap tightly);
yo, [k1, p1] 3 times, w&t; [k1, p1] 3 times, w&t (wrap tightly);
yo, [k1, p1] twice, w&t; [k1, p1] twice, w&t (wrap tightly);
yo, k1, p1, w&t; k1, p1, w&t (wrap tightly);
yo, [k1, p1] 5 times, hiding wraps, and ending at outside edge–29 sts.
Row 11: BO 9 sts in rib pattern, p1, [k1, p1] 9 times (do not hide wraps)–20 sts remain.
Repeat Rows 1-11 until piece measures 58", ending with Row 7. Repeat Rows 1 and 2 once. BO all sts in pattern

two-tone vest

LYNNE BARR

Embrace your eccentric side by wearing this vest with the cutout side in front (see page 100). For a more conservative but very flattering empire style, wear the opposite side to the front (see right). The provisional cast-on at the shoulders, and the use of slipped stitches when changing colors while working a rib pattern, creates a vest with no wrong side.

SIZES
X-Small (Small, Medium, Large, X-Large)
To fit bust sizes 28-30 (32-34, 36-38, 40-42, 44-46)"
Shown in size Small

FINISHED MEASUREMENTS
24½ (27½, 30, 32¾, 35½)" chest, unstretched
Note: The ribbing will stretch significantly. This top is meant to fit very close. If you prefer a less close fit, you may wish to work the next size larger.

YARN
Rowan Yarns Felted Tweed (50% merino wool / 25% alpaca / 25% viscose/rayon; 190 yards / 50 grams): 1 (2, 2, 2, 2) balls #152 Watery (A); 2 (2, 2, 2, 2) balls #153 Phantom (B)

NEEDLES
Two 20" (50 cm) long or longer circular (circ) needles size US 4 (3.5 mm)
One set of three double-pointed needles (dpn) size US 4 (3.5 mm)
One 20" (50 cm) long or longer circular needle size US 5 (3.75 mm)
Change needle size if necessary to obtain correct gauge.

NOTIONS
Waste yarn; stitch holders; removable marker; stitch markers in 2 colors

GAUGE
34½ sts and 34 rows = 4" (10 cm) in K1, P1 Rib, using smaller needles, unstretched

NOTES
This Vest is reversible not only by turning it inside out, but also by turning it back to front. For the purposes of the instructions, the shallower neck will be in the front, and the deeper neck will be in the back. The piece is worked from the top down. The Back Straps are worked separately, beginning with a Provisional CO. Then the Front Straps are picked up from the Provisional CO and worked down to the neck. The Back is joined to the Front briefly to complete the Bodice, then worked separately until the Back Chest Band shaping is completed. The Front and Back are worked back and forth until the Back vee is complete, then worked in the round to the bottom edge.

BODICE

BACK STRAPS (make 2)

Using dpns, waste yarn, and Provisional CO (see page 178), CO 20 (22, 24, 26, 28) sts. Change to A; knit 1 row. Work in K1, P1, Rib, slipping first knit st of each row knitwise, until piece measures 5 (5½, 6, 6½, 7)" from the beginning.

Shape Armhole: Increase 2 sts this row, then every other row 3 times, as follows: Slip 1 knitwise, p1, AO-h 2 sts, work to end—28 (30, 32, 34, 36) sts. Transfer sts to st holder.

FRONT STRAPS (make 2)

Carefully unravel Provisional CO and place sts on dpn, being careful not to twist sts; place removable marker for top of shoulder. Using A, work in K1, P1 Rib, slipping first knit st of each row knitwise, until piece measures 4¼ (4, 4¼, 4½, 4½)" from top of shoulder, ending with armhole sts at left-hand end of needle.

Note: Work all increased sts in rib pattern as they become available.

Shape Neck and Armhole: Increase 2 sts this row, then every row 6 times, as follows: Slip 1 knitwise, p1, AO-h 2 sts, work to end—34 (36, 38, 40, 42) sts. Set aside.

Join Front Sides: Transfer both Front Sides to smaller circ needle, with armholes at outside edges, and neck edges in the center. *Note: Before transferring sts, you will have to turn one Front Side over so that Fronts are now mirror images.* Using yarn attached to first side (break yarn at other edge), slip 1, p1, AO-h 2 sts, work to end of first side, CO 26 (26, 30, 30, 30) sts for center neck, work across second side to end—96 (100, 108, 112, 116) sts.

Shape Armhole: Increase 2 sts at beginning of next 5 (11, 13, 15, 21) rows, as follows: Slip 1, p1, AO-h 2 sts, work to end—106 (122, 134, 142, 158) sts.

Join Front to Back Straps: Work to end of Front, work across Back Strap sts from st holder.

Repeat last row once—162 (182, 198, 210, 230) sts. Work even until piece measures 3¼ (3½, 3¾, 4, 4¼)" from end of armhole shaping. Transfer first and last 22 (24, 26, 28, 30) sts to separate dpns for Back Strap. Leave remaining center 118 (134, 146, 154, 170) sts on circ needle for Body.

BACK CHEST BAND

Notes: 1) Chest Band will be shaped using Short Rows (see Short-Row Shaping, page 186). 2) When shaping the Back Chest Band, in each pair of rows, you will work a specified number of sts on the first row, w&t then work back to the edge on the second row. 3) On all following rows, work each wrap together with its wrapped st as you come to it.

Continuing on dpn with yarn attached (set aside other dpn for grafting), work even for 1 row, slipping first st of row knitwise.

SHAPE STRAP CURVE

Rows 1 and 2: Work 3 sts, w&t; work to end.

Rows 3 and 4: Work to 3 sts past wrapped st from previous row, w&t; work to end.

Repeat Rows 3 and 4 two (three, three, four, four) times.

Rows 5 and 6: Work 5 sts, w&t; work to end.

Rows 7 and 8: Work to 3 sts past wrapped st from previous row, w&t; work to end.

Repeat Rows 7 and 8 two (two, three, three, four) times.

END STRAP CURVE

Place removable marker at beginning of row. Work even until piece measures 3¾ (4½, 4¾, 5½, 5¾)" from marker, ending at outer edge of Band. *Note: When you have worked 1⅞ (2¼, 2⅜, 2¾, 2⅞)", try the Vest on to make sure the Chest Band reaches center of back or front. Adjust length of work-even section if necessary.*

Repeat Strap Curve shaping. Work even for 1 row.

Using Kitchener st for K1, P1 Rib (see page 183), graft live end of Band to sts on hold on opposite side of Bodice.

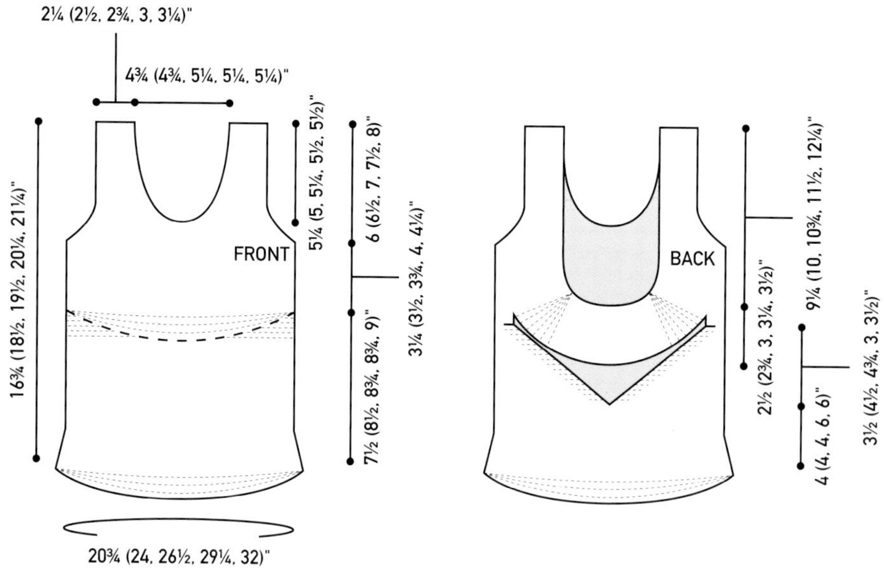
2¼ (2½, 2¾, 3, 3¼)"
4¾ (4¾, 5¼, 5¼, 5¼)"
16¾ (18½, 19½, 20¼, 21¼)"
FRONT
5¼ (5, 5¼, 5½, 5½)"
6 (6½, 7, 7½, 8)"
3¼ (3½, 3¾, 4, 4¼)"
7½ (8½, 8¾, 8¾, 9)"
20¾ (24, 26½, 29¼, 32)"
BACK
9¼ (10, 10¾, 11½, 12¼)"
2½ (2¾, 3, 3¼, 3½)"
3½ (4½, 4¾, 3, 3½)"
4 (4, 4, 6, 6)"

Note: Piece is worked from the top down. The fine dotted lines indicate short-row shaping sections.

SHAPE LOWER FRONT BODICE

Note: Lower Front Bodice will be shaped using Short Rows.
Rejoin A to sts for Front Bodice on hold on circ needle.

Rows 1 and 2: [Work to last 3 sts, w&t] twice.
Rows 3 and 4: [Work to last 5 sts, w&t] twice.
Rows 5 and 6: [Work to last 9 sts, w&t] twice.
Rows 7 and 8: [Work to last 13 sts, w&t] twice.
Rows 9 and 10: [Work to last 17 sts, w&t] twice.
Rows 11 and 12: [Work to last 23 sts, w&t] twice.
Rows 13 and 14: [Work to last 29 sts, w&t] twice.
Rows 15 and 16: Work across all sts, hiding all wraps on first row as you come to them.

BODY

JOIN FRONT AND BACK

Note: To change colors and work a reversible rib, the first rnd in the new color is worked with all knit sts being knit and all purl sts being slipped; the second rnd is worked with all knit sts being slipped and all purl sts being purled. All sts are slipped purlwise.

Join B to Front Bodice sts at right side edge. Using smaller circ needle, *k1, slip 1 wyif; repeat from * to end, place marker (pm) for left side and beginning of rnd, using Knitted Cast-On (see page 178), CO 62 (78, 82, 98, 106) sts for Back, pm for right side–180 (212, 228, 252, 276) sts. Join for working in the rnd, *slip 1 purlwise wyib, p1; repeat from * to beginning-of-rnd marker. Work even for 1 rnd, working Back CO sts in K1, P1 rib.

SHAPE BACK

Left Side

Note: The short rows will be worked back and forth on either side of beginning-of-rnd marker when working left side, and on either side of side marker when working Right Side. Slip marker as you come to it. Hide all wraps as you come to them.

Rows 1 (RS) and 2: Work 2 (2, 2, 4, 4) sts, w&t; work to 8 sts past marker, w&t.
Rows 3 and 4: Work to 1 (1, 1, 3, 3) st(s) past wrapped st of previous row, w&t; work to 18 sts past marker, w&t.

Rows 5 and 6: Work to 1 (1, 1, 3, 3) st(s) past wrapped st of previous row, w&t; work to 30 sts past marker, w&t.

Rows 7 and 8: Work to 1 (1, 1, 3, 3) st(s) past wrapped st of previous row, w&t; work across Front sts to side marker. Do not turn.

Right Side

Rows 1 (WS) and 2: Work 1 (1, 1, 3, 3) st(s), w&t; work to 9 sts past marker, w&t.

Rows 3 and 4: Work to 1 (1, 1, 3, 3) st(s) past wrapped st of previous row, w&t; work to 19 sts past marker, w&t.

Rows 5 and 6: Work to 1 (1, 1, 3, 3) st(s) past wrapped st of previous row, w&t; work to 31 sts past marker, w&t.

Rows 7 and 8: Work to 1 (1, 1, 3, 3) st(s) past wrapped st of previous row, w&t; work across Front sts to beginning-of-rnd marker. Do not turn.

Both Sides

Rows 9 (RS) and 10: Work 10 (10, 10, 20, 20) sts, w&t; work to 9 (9, 9, 19, 19) sts past side marker, w&t.

Row 11: Work to 1 (1, 1, 3, 3) sts past wrapped st of previous row, w&t.

Repeat Row 11 until you reach the center Back purl st, with no sts left to wrap, turn; work to beginning-of-rnd marker. Join for working in the rnd. Work even until piece measures 1½" from end of short-row shaping.

Next Row: Change to larger needles. Work even until piece measures 4 (4, 4, 6, 6)" from end of short-row shaping. Shift markers 14 (14, 16, 14, 16) sts toward the Front on either side, so there are now 90 (106, 114, 126, 138) sts between markers on Front and Back. Left side marker is now beginning-of-rnd marker.

SHAPE BODY

Front

Rows 1 (RS) and 2: Work to 4 sts before new beginning-of-rnd marker, w&t; work to 4 sts before new right side marker, w&t.

Rows 3 and 4: [Work to 4 sts before wrapped st of last row, w&t] twice.

Rows 5 and 6: Repeat Rows 3 and 4.

Rows 7 and 8: [Work to 8 sts before wrapped st of last row, w&t] twice.

Rows 9 and 10: Repeat Rows 7 and 8.

Row 11: Work across all sts to beginning-of-rnd marker, hiding all wraps as you come to them; do not turn.

Back

Rows 1 and 2: Work to 4 sts before right side marker, w&t; work to 4 sts before beginning-of-rnd marker, w&t.

Repeat Rows 3-11 of Front shaping, ending at side marker. Working in the rnd, work even for 1 rnd, ending back at side marker. BO all sts in rib.

investments

CAT BORDHI

With a witty name for a playful yet seriously creative idea, Cat's vest is truly an asset in many ways. The two interchangeable and reversible pieces allow for versatility in the way the vest is worn. Wear two overlapping pieces for extra winter warmth, or put on just a single piece for a fashion-forward one-shouldered style in less chilly weather.

SIZES
Small/Medium (Medium/Large)
To fit bust sizes 32-38 (40-46)"

YARN
Frog Tree Alpaca Sport (100% alpaca; 130 yards / 50 grams):
7 (9) skeins each #00 (A) and #20 (B)

NEEDLES
One 24" (60 cm) long or longer circular (circ) needle size
US 7 (4.5 mm)
One pair double-pointed needles (dpn) size US 7 (4.5 mm)
Change needle size if necessary to obtain correct gauge.

NOTIONS
Stitch markers in 4 colors; stitch holders

GAUGE
19 sts and 34 rows = 4" (10 cm) in Garter stitch (knit every row),
using 2 strands of yarn held together

NOTES
The Vest is worked in 2 Vest Halves, each exactly alike, but in 2 different colors. Each Vest Half is made up of Panels A, B, and C. Panel A has a square base; Panel B has diagonal shaping along the left-hand edge of the base. Both Panels are worked separately and shaped along one edge to form a Shoulder Strap; the Straps meet in the center of the shoulder, where they are joined and worked together to form 1 piece. Panel C is worked in 2 pieces to begin, each piece picked up from either Panel A or B. The Panel C pieces are then joined and worked to the end, working together with sts from each of the other Panels so that the 3 Panels are joined together to form the underarm section of the Vest Half.

VEST

VEST HALF (make 2, 1 in each color)
Notes: 1) All Panels are worked in Garter stitch (knit every row) throughout. The instructions will list only those rows on which there is an increase or decrease. Knit all other rows. 2) For ease of working each size, the first set of row numbers applies to size Small/Medium; the second set of row numbers (within brackets) applies to size Medium/Large. Where there is only one set of row numbers, it applies to both sizes.

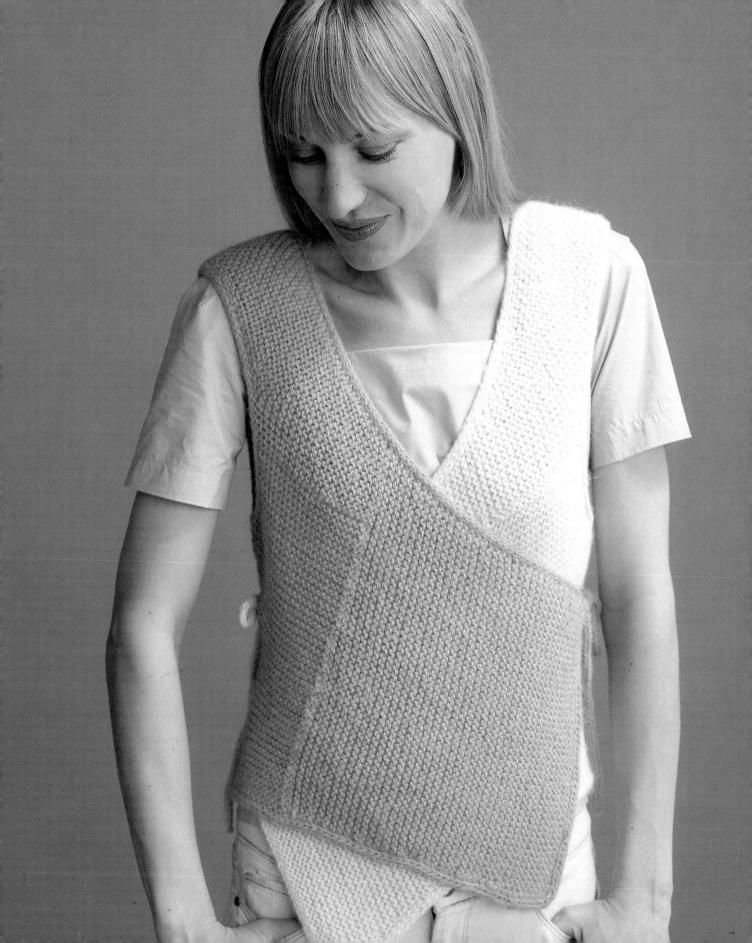

Panel A

Base

With circ needle and 2 strands of yarn held together, CO 49 (57) sts. Begin Garter st (knit every row).

Knit all rows from 1-120 (138), except those listed below:

Rows 20, 40, and 60 [18, 36, 54, and 72]: Skp, knit to end.

Rows 23, 37, 45, 53, 61, 67, 71, and 75 [23, 37, 45, 53, 61, 69, 75, 81, and 85]: K1-f/b, knit to end–54 (62) sts after Row 75 [85].

Shoulder Strap

Row 79 [89]: K1-f/b, k10 (12), turn, placing remaining 43 (49) sts on holder–12 (14) sts remain.

Rows 83, 87, 91, 95, 97, 101, 105, 107, 111, 113, 115, 117, and 119 [93, 97, 101, 105, 107, 111, 115, 117, 121, 125, 129, 131, 133, 135, and 137]: K1-f/b, knit to end–25 (29) sts after Row 119 [137].

Row 121 [139]: K1-f/b, k18, turn, placing last 6 (10) sts on holder–20 sts remain.

Row 122 [140] and all Even-Numbered Rows through Row 140 [160]: Skp, knit to end.

Row 123 [141] and all Odd-Numbered Rows through Row 141 [161]: K1-f/b, knit to end.

Place sts on holder; set aside.

Panel B

Base

With circ needle and 2 strands of yarn held together, CO 63 (71) sts. Begin Garter st (knit every row).

Knit all rows from 1-120 (138), except those listed below:

Rows 2, 4, 6, 10, 12, 16, 20, 22, 26, 28, 32, 38, 44, 50, 56, 62, and 68 [2, 4, 6, 10, 14, 18, 20, 24, 28, 30, 34, 40, 46, 52, 58, 64, 70, and 76]: Skp, knit to end.

Rows 23, 37, 45, 53, 61, 67, 71, and 75 [23, 37, 45, 53, 61, 69, 75, 81, and 85]: K1-f/b, knit to end–54 (62) sts after Row 75 [85].

Complete as for Panel A through Row 141 [161].

Row 142 [162]: Knit to end. Break yarn.

Join Panels at Shoulders

Lay both Panels flat, with Base of Panel A on the right, Base of Panel B on the left, and the Shoulder Straps of both Panels meeting in the center (see Step 1). Transfer 20 Panel A Shoulder Strap sts to right-hand end of circ needle, before Panel B Shoulder Strap sts; place marker (pm) A between the 2 sets of sts–40 sts.

Row 1: With 2 strands of yarn held together, working across all sts, knit to 2 sts before marker, skp, knit to last 2 sts, skp–38 sts remain.

Rows 2-19: Repeat Row 1–2 sts remain after Row 19 (see Step 2).

Row 20: Skp–1 st remains. Break yarn and fasten off.

Panel C

First Side

Beginning at top corner of straight edge of Panel A Shoulder Strap, and ending just above 43 (49) sts on holder for Panel A, with separate needle, pick up (but do not knit) 21 (24) sts (1 st in each purl ridge). Pm A before last st. Transfer 43 (49) sts from holder to separate needle (see Step 3).

Row 1 and all Odd-Numbered Rows through Row 15 [17]: With circ needle and 2 strands of yarn held together, knit to marker, skp (last st on needle together with 1 st from Panel A needle), turn–56 (64) sts remain after Row 15 [17].

Row 2 and all Even-Numbered Rows through Row 28 [32]: Knit.

Row 17 [19] and all Odd-Numbered Rows through Row 29 [33]: K1-f/b, knit to marker, skp (last st on needle together with 1 st from Panel A needle), turn. Place sts on holder; set aside.

Second Side

Work as for First Side through Row 29 [33], picking up sts from Panel B instead of Panel A. Use different colored marker (marker C).

Row 30 [34]: Knit. Break yarn.

Join Panel C Sides

Turn pieces over so Panel A is on the right and Panel B on the left, with the Shoulder Strap facing you, and the CO edges of both pieces facing away from you. Transfer all sts (including markers) to one circ needle as follows: 28 (32) sts from edge of Panel A, First Side Panel C sts, pm B, Second Side panel C sts, 28 (32) sts from edge of Panel B–112 (128) sts. Now transfer 28 (32) sts from edge of Panel A to opposite end of needle, ready to work on First Side Panel C sts (see Step 4).

Row 1 and all Odd-Numbered Rows through Row 11: Knit to 2 sts before B, skp, knit to C, skp, turn.

Row 2 and all Even-Numbered Rows though Row 12: Knit to 2 sts before B, skp, knit to A, skp, turn–88 (104) sts remain after Row 12.

Side Slit

Row 13: Knit to 2 sts before B, skp, join 2 new strands of yarn held together, knit to C, skp, turn.

Row 14: Working both sides at the same time, changing yarn at B, knit to 2 sts before B, skp, knit to A, skp, turn.

Rows 15-20 [22]: Repeat Rows 13 and 14–36 (42) sts remain each side after Row 20 [22]. Break new strands.

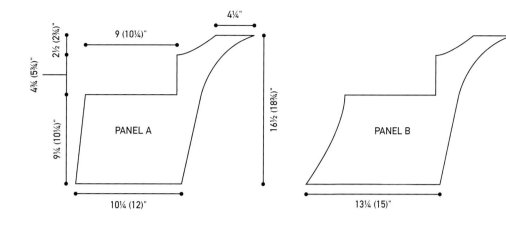

Diagram labels:
- 2½ (2¾)"
- 9 (10¼)"
- 4¼"
- 4¾ (5¾)"
- 9¼ (10¼)"
- PANEL A
- 16½ (18¾)"
- 10¼ (12)"
- PANEL B
- 13¼ (15)"

Rejoin Sides

Rows 21, 23, 25, 29, 37, and 45 [23, 25, 27, 31, 39, 47, and 55]: Working across all sts with same yarn, repeat Row 1.

Rows 22, 24, 26, 30, 38, and 46 [24, 26, 28, 32, 40, 48, and 56]: Repeat Row 2.

Rows 27-28, 31-36, 39-44, and 47-56 [29-30, 33-38, 41-46, 49-54, and 57-62]: Knit to third marker (A or C), skp, turn–24 (30) sts remain after Row 56 [62]. Break yarn. Place sts on holder. Set aside.

I-Cord Ties and Top Border

With dpn, CO 3 sts.

Work Free I-Cord: *Transfer needle with sts to left hand, bring yarn around behind work to right-hand side; using second dpn, knit sts from right to left, pulling yarn from left to right for first st; do not turn. Slide sts to opposite end of needle; repeat from * until piece measures 10", or to desired length for Tie. Set aside; do not break yarn.

Work Attached I-Cord: With circ needle, pick up (but do not knit) 1 st for each purl ridge along top edge of Vest Half, working from CO edge of Panel B, over shoulder join, to CO edge of Panel A (see Step 5). Transfer live I-Cord sts to left-hand needle, in front of first picked-up st; yarn should be coming from third I-Cord st.

*K2, skp (last st from I-Cord together with 1 picked-up st); slide sts back to beginning of needle; repeat from * until all picked-up sts have been worked. Continue working Free I-Cord for 10", or to desired length for Tie. Break yarn, thread through remaining sts, pull tight and fasten off.

Bottom I-Cord Border

With circ needle, pick up (but do not knit) 1 st for each purl ridge along remaining edges of Vest Half and place markers as follows: Beginning with Panel A, pick up sts to end of CO row, pm A, work to Panel C sts on holder, pm B, transfer Panel C sts to needle, pm C, work to end of CO row of Panel B, pm D, work to opposite end of CO row of Panel B (see Step 5).

With dpn, beginning at Attached I-Cord on Panel A, pick up and knit 3 sts from underside of Attached I-Cord; work Attached I-Cord to A; at A, work 1 row of Free I-Cord, 1 row of Attached, then 1 row of Free; between A and B, repeat [4 rows of Attached, then 1 row of Free]; between B and C, work Attached; between C and D, repeat [2 rows of Attached, then 1 row of Free]; at D, work 2 rows of Free I-Cord, 1 row of Attached, then 2 rows of Free; between D and end of picked-up sts, work Attached I-Cord. Sew remaining live sts into underside of Top I-Cord Border.

Armhole I-Cord Border

With circ needle, beginning at bottom center of armhole, pick up (but do not knit) 1 st for each purl ridge around entire armhole edge, including sts on holders. With dpn, CO 3 sts. Work Attached I-Cord around armhole edge. Graft ends of I-Cord together using Kitchener st (see page 183). *Note: If you prefer, you may sew the ends together.*

FINISHING

Weave in all ends.

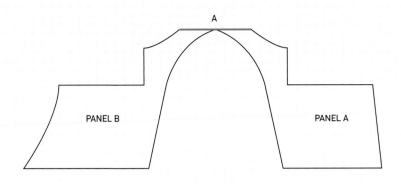

STEP 1

Transfer sts from holder
for Panel A to end of needle
holding Panel B sts (blue line);
place marker A between 2
sets of sts.

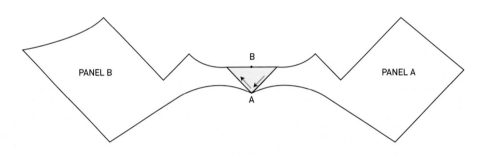

STEP 2

Decrease 1 st at A and 1 st
at end of row. Follow direction
of arrows for odd-numbered
rows; work in opposite
direction for even-numbered
rows. Working a decrease
at point A on every row will
shape the area between the
two Panels into a triangle
(tan shaded area). The last st
will be at point B.

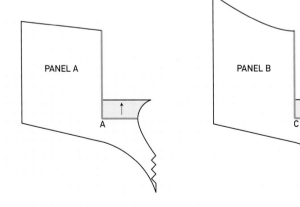

STEP 3

Pick up sts along straight
edge of Panel A or B (orange
line). Transfer 43 (49) sts on
holder for Panel (green line) to
separate needle. Work Panel
C (tan shaded area), shaping
right-hand side, and working
1 st from Panel C together with
one st from Panel A or B, as
appropriate.

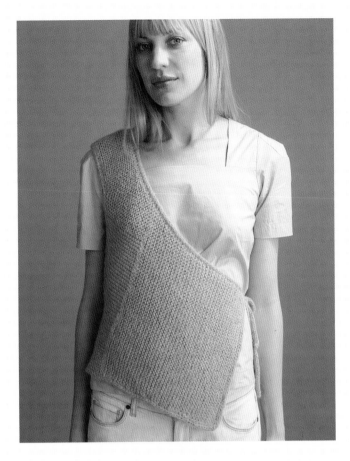

Transfer all sts to same needle, as follows (green line): E to A sts, A to B sts, B to C sts, then C to F sts. Now transfer E to A sts to opposite end of needle, ready to work on A to B sts. Work A to C as instructed, for 8 rows. Work side slit, then continue as established to end of Panel C.

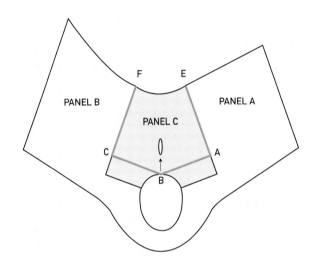

STEP 5

Work Top I-Cord Border along orange line. Work Bottom I-Cord Border along purple line, working Free or Attached I-Cord as indicated at or between points A, B, C, and D.

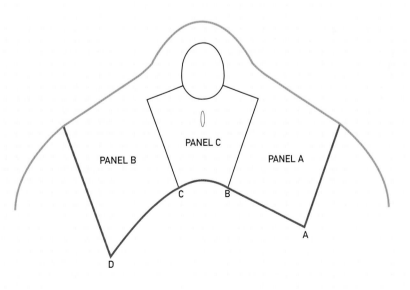

double-knit vest

LYNNE BARR

Traditional and contemporary elements come together to create a classic-style vest with a fresh modern feel. One rectangular double-knit piece encircles the neck, creating a yoke with seamless shoulders and collar. Working downward from live stitches on the collar yoke, the back shoulders are fashionably narrow, creating a decidedly feminine look. The double-knit yoke sports the Lattice Border and Checks pattern (see page 82), two completely different patterns on opposing sides–a bold check on one side (shown at right), and a solid with delicate lattice border on the other (below).

SIZES

X-Small (Small, Medium, Large, X-Large)
To fit bust sizes 28-30 (32-34, 36-38, 40-42, 44-46)"
Shown in size Small

FINISHED MEASUREMENTS

31 (35, 38¾, 42¾, 45½)" chest, stretched
Note: The ribbing will stretch significantly. This top is meant to fit very close. If you prefer a less close fit, you may wish to work the next size larger.

YARN

Rowan Yarns Felted Tweed (50% merino wool/25% alpaca/25% viscose/rayon; 190 yards / 50 grams): 4 (5, 5, 6, 7) balls #152 Watery (MC); 1 (1, 1, 2, 2) balls #156 Wheat (CC)

NEEDLES

One 32" (80 cm) long circular (circ) needle size US 6 (4 mm)
Two 16" (40 cm) long circular needles size US 6 (4 mm)
or smaller, to BO sts
One 24" (60 cm) long or longer circular needle size US 8 (5 mm)
Two 16" (40 cm) long circular needles size US 8 (5 mm), to pick up sts
Change needle size if necessary to obtain correct gauge.

NOTIONS

Stitch markers in 3 colors

GAUGE

39 sts and 27 rows = 4" (10 cm) in Lattice Border and Checks pattern from Chart, using smaller needles and 1 strand of yarn
22 sts and 24 rows = 4" (10 cm) in K1, P1 Rib, using larger needles and 2 strands of yarn held together, unstretched
16½ sts and 23 rows = 4" (10 cm) in K1, P1 Rib, using larger needles and 2 strands of yarn held together, stretched

STITCH PATTERN

K1, P1 RIB

(multiple of 2 sts; 1-row/rnd repeat)

Row/Rnd 1: *K1, p1; repeat from * to end [end k1 if an odd number of sts].

Row/Rnd 2: Knit the knit sts and purl the purl sts as they face you. Repeat Row/Rnd 2 for K1, P1 Rib.

NOTES

The Vest is totally reversible. However, for the purposes of the instructions, one side will be labeled RS and the other side WS. The Front Yoke/Collar is one long piece which wraps around the back neck to the front, over the shoulders. The cast-on edge of the Front Yoke/Collar forms the top of the back collar and the inside edges of the neckline. The stitches in the center portion of the bound-off edge are left live, and the Back is worked down from these stitches. The bound-off side sections of the Front Yoke/Collar form the armhole edges of the Front Yoke, and the two side (narrow) edges of the Front Yoke/Collar form a base from which stitches for the rest of the Front are picked up.

VEST

FRONT YOKE/COLLAR

Notes: 1) When MC and CC yarns are on the same edge, twist yarns at the beginning of the row (see Double Knitting, page 181). 2) When slipping sts, slip knit sts knitwise and purl sts purlwise.
Using Cable Cast-On (see page 178), 32" circ needle and MC, CO 216 (224, 232, 240, 248) sts.

Next Row (RS): Begin Lattice Border and Checks pattern (see page 82). Work Rows 1-14 once, then repeat Rows 11-14 until piece measures 5 (5½, 6, 6½, 7)" from the beginning.

Next Row (RS): Change to MC and work K1, P1 Rib for 1 row.

Using the 2 smaller 16" circ needles, divide first 78 (82, 84, 88, 90) sts (see Divide Stitches, page 185), slipping knit sts to front needle and purl sts to back needle. With MC and Kitchener st (see page 183), BO the divided sts. On opposite end of Yoke, divide last 78 (82, 84, 88, 90) sts and BO in the same manner, leaving center 60 (60, 64, 64, 68) sts on needle for Back.

BACK

Next Row (RS): Using 2 strands of MC held together, work K1, P1 Rib across Back sts, decreasing 3 sts evenly spaced across row, working decreases as k2tog or p2tog, as appropriate for rib–57 (57, 61, 61, 65) sts remain. Work even for 2 rows, slipping first st of each row.

Next Row (WS): Change to 24" circ needle and continue to work even, slipping first st of each row, until piece measures 5¼ (5¼, 5¼, 5¼, 5½)" from end of Yoke, ending with a WS row.

Shape Armholes

Notes: 1) Armholes are shaped using short rows (see Short-Row Shaping, page 186). 2) Work increased sts in rib pattern as they become available.

Size X-Small Only

Next Row (RS): Slip 1, p1, AO-h 1 st, rib 18 sts, w&t; rib to last 2 sts, AO-h 1 st, k1, p1;

slip 1, p1, AO-h 1 st, rib 12 sts, w&t; rib to last 2 sts, AO-h 1 st, k1, p1;

slip 1, rib to end, hiding wraps;

slip 1, k1, AO-h 1 st, rib 18 sts, w&t; rib to last 2 sts, AO-h 1 st, p1, k1;

slip 1, k1, AO-h 1 st, rib 12 sts, w&t; rib to last 2 sts, AO-h 1 st, p1, k1;

slip 1, k1, rib to end, hiding wraps–65 sts.

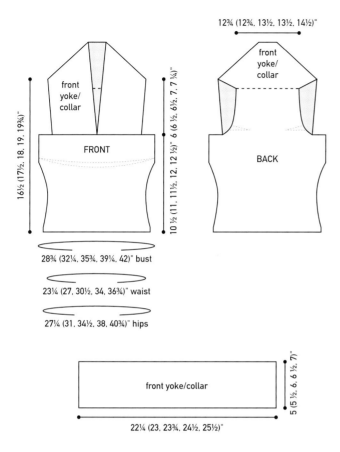

12¾ (12¾, 13½, 13½, 14½)"

front yoke/collar

FRONT

16½ (17½, 18, 19, 19¾)"

10½ (11, 11½, 12, 12½)"
6 (6½, 6½, 7, 7¼)"

28¾ (32¼, 35¾, 39¼, 42)" bust

23¼ (27, 30½, 34, 36¾)" waist

27¼ (31, 34½, 38, 40¾)" hips

front yoke/collar

BACK

front yoke/collar

5 (5½, 6, 6½, 7)"

22¼ (23, 23¾, 24½, 25½)"

Note: Front Yoke/Collar is worked first. Center Back is worked from live sts at center of Front Yoke/Collar, down to armhole. Front is picked up from bottom (narrow) edges of Front Yoke/Collar. Back and Front are joined at the armholes and worked in the round to bottom edge. The dotted lines at front bust and back armholes indicate short-row shaping sections.

Sizes (Small, Medium, Large, X-Large) only

Next Row (RS): Slip 1, p1, AO-h 1 st, rib 18 sts, w&t; rib to last 2 sts, AO-h 1 st, k1, p1;

slip 1, p1, AO-h 1 st, rib 12 sts, w&t; rib to last 2 sts, AO-h 1 st, k1, p1;

slip 1, p1, AO-h 1 st, rib to last 2 sts, hiding wraps, AO-h 1 st, p1, k1;

slip 1, k1, AO-h 1 st, rib 18 sts, w&t; rib to last 2 sts, AO-h 1 st, p1, k1;

slip 1, k1, AO-h 1 st, rib 12 sts, w&t; rib to last 2 sts, AO-h 1 st, p1, k1;

slip 1, k1, AO-h 1 st, rib to last 2 sts, hiding wraps, AO-h 1 st, k1, p1.

Row 1 (RS): Slip 1, p1, AO-h 1 st, rib to last 2 sts, AO-h 1 st, p1, k1.

Row 2: Slip 1, k1, AO-h 1 st, rib to last 2 sts, AO-h 1 st, k1, p1.

Repeat Rows 1 and 2 (zero, zero, one, one) time(s)–(73, 77, 81, 85) sts.

All Sizes

Next Row (RS): Rib to end, place marker (pm) A for right side, AO-f 4 (6, 8, 12, 14) sts for underarm–69 (79, 85, 93, 99) sts.

JOIN BACK AND FRONTS

Note: When picking up sts, only pick up the edge half of the stitch (one thread), making sure the half that you pick up is from the side that is facing you.

Next Row (RS) Using larger 16" circ needle and 1 strand of yarn from Back, pick up and knit 28 (30, 34, 36, 38) sts along bottom (narrow edge) of Front Yoke, turn work; with same strand and second larger 16" circ needle, working on opposite side from first pick-ups, pick up and knit 28 (30, 34, 36, 38) sts along bottom of same Front Yoke, turn work. With both strands of yarn held together, using 32" circ needle, work picked-up sts as follows: *P2tog (1 st from front needle together with 1 st from back needle), k2tog (1 st from front needle together with 1 st from back needle); repeat from * to end–28 (30, 34, 36, 38) sts. Work second half of Front Yoke as for first. Do not turn. AO-f 3 (5, 7, 11, 13) sts, pm B for left side, AO-f 1 st. Join for working in the rnd; slip last AO st to left-hand needle, k2tog (AO st with first st of Back), work to A (beginning of rnd)–128 (144, 160, 176, 188) sts. Work even until piece measures 2½" from base of Yoke.

Shape Bust: Work to 2 sts before B, w&t; work to 2 sts before A, w&t;

work to 6 sts before B, w&t; work to 6 sts from A, w&t.

Next Rnd: Work across all sts, hiding wraps as you come to them. Work even until piece measures 3 (3, 3½, 4, 4½)" from base of Yoke. *Note: You may adjust the length here if necessary, to make sure that you begin waist shaping 3½" above your waist.*

Shape Waist: Work to B, work 12 (14, 14, 16, 16) sts, pm C, [work 16 (18, 20, 22, 24) sts, pm C] twice, work to A.

Decrease Rnd: Decrease 3 sts this rnd, then every other rnd 7 times, as follows: [Work to next C marker, slip marker (sm), ssk] 3 times, work to end–104 (120, 136, 152, 164) sts remain. Work even for 1".

Increase Rnd: Increase 3 sts this rnd, then every 4 rnds 5 times, as follows: [Work to next C marker, k1, AO-h 1 st] 3 times, work to end–122 (138, 154, 170, 182) sts. Work even until piece measures 10½ (11, 11½, 12, 12½)" from underarm.

Using 2 smaller circ needles, BO all sts using K1, P1 Bind-Off with Kitchener (see page 184). *Note: You may work the bind-off in sections rather than dividing all the sts at once. If you have spare dpns, you may use those rather than the circulars.*

TEVA DURHAM

geometric dress

Teva has taken stripes to a whole new level, and they couldn't be any more striking than they are in this dress. Worked in the round using slipped stitches, the maze of nested angular stripes creates a bold and beautiful mosaic on the knit side (see right). Flipped to the purl side, the pattern takes on a slightly softer woven look (see page 117).

SIZES
Small/Medium (Large)

FINISHED MEASUREMENTS
34 (40)" chest

YARN
Loop-d-Loop by Teva Durham River (90% cotton / 10% cashmere; 103 yards / 50 grams): 5 (6) balls #03 Coffee (A)
Loop-d-Loop by Teva Durham Birch (90% cotton / 10% silk; 98 yards / 50 grams): 5 (6) balls #03 Dove Grey (B)

NEEDLES
One 29" (74 cm) long circular (circ) needle size US 8 (5 mm)
One 16" (40 cm) long circular needle size US 7 (4.5 mm)
Change needle size if necessary to obtain correct gauge.

NOTIONS
Stitch holders; stitch marker

GAUGE
14 sts and 20 rows = 4" (10 cm) over pattern from Chart A, using larger needles

NOTES
The Dress is worked in rounds from hem to armholes, then Front and Back are worked separately to shoulders. The Dress is reversible. However, for the purposes of the instructions, one side will be labeled RS and the other side WS.

SKIRT
Using larger needle and A, CO 144 (168) sts. Join for working in the rnd, being careful not to twist sts; place marker for beginning of rnd. Knit 1 rnd. Change to A; begin Chart A, changing colors as indicated. Work Rnds 1-50 once, then Rnds 3-47 once.

Shape Waist
Next Rnd: Change to Chart B. Work Rnds 1-3 once, working decreases as indicated in Chart–120 (140) sts remain. Work Rnds 4-43 once, then Rnds 4-11 once.

BACK
DIVIDE FOR BACK AND FRONT
Next Rnd: Continuing Chart B, Rnd 12, work 60 sts, transfer last 60 (70) sts worked to holder for Front; work to end–60 (70) sts remain. Working back and forth, work even for 1 row.

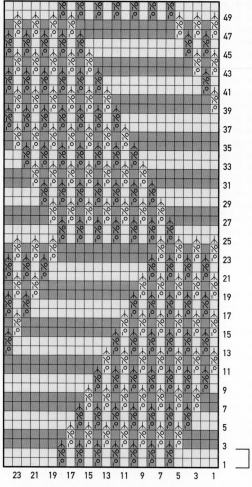

49
47
45
43
41
39
37
35
33
31
29
27
25
23
21
19
17
15
13
11
9
7
5
3
1

23 21 19 17 15 13 11 9 7 5 3 1

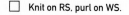
Set-Up Rnds – do not repeat

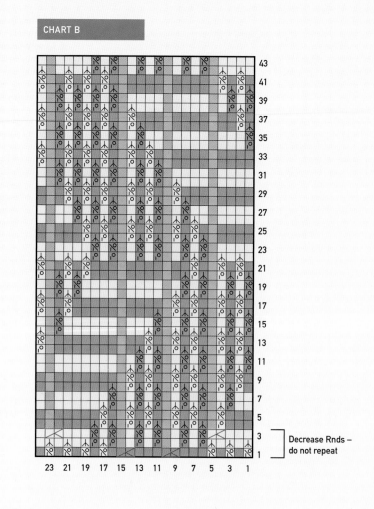

43
41
39
37
35
33
31
29
27
25
23
21
19
17
15
13
11
9
7
5
3
1

23 21 19 17 15 13 11 9 7 5 3 1

Decrease Rnds – do not repeat

KEY

☐ Knit on RS, purl on WS.

▨ A

☐ B

⌐°⌐ Yo, slip 1 st (opposite color) purlwise.

⌐⊠⌐ On RS, yo, slip 2 sts purlwise (1 st in opposite color, and yo in working color from previous rnd/row) purlwise; on WS, slip 2 sts purlwise, yo.

⅄ K3tog (1 st in working color together with 2 yo's in opposite color).

⧄ K2tog (only when indicated in pattern text).

▨ No stitch

CHART NOTES

1. Alternate 2 rnds/rows in A, then 2 rnds/rows in B throughout Chart.

2. Where you have B squares in the Chart on an A rnd/row, you will be slipping the B sts, and vice versa.

3. All yo's on the RS are worked by bringing the yarn to the front before slipping the st(s), and letting the yo create itself when the k1 or k3tog is worked. Yo's are not made by wrapping the yarn over the top of the needle and to the back again. Yo's on the WS are worked by bringing the yarn over the needle to the back, then under the needle to the front.

Shape Armhole: Work Rows 14-43 once, then repeat Rows 4-43 for remainder of Dress and AT THE SAME TIME, decrease 1 st each side this row, then every other row 14 (17) times–30 (34) sts remain. Work even until armholes measure 7 (7½)" from beginning of shaping, ending with a WS row. BO all sts.

FRONT

With WS facing, join yarn at underarm. Work as for Back until armholes measure 6½ (7)" from beginning of shaping, ending with a WS row.

Shape Neck (RS): Work 8 sts, join a second ball of yarn, BO center 14 (18) sts, work to end. Working both sides at the same time, decrease 1 st at each neck edge every other row twice–6 sts remain each side for shoulders. Work even, alternating colors as in Chart, but working only in St st, for 3", ending with a WS row. BO all sts. *Note: Front armhole edge will be longer than Back armhole edge, so that shoulder straps fall to back of shoulder.*

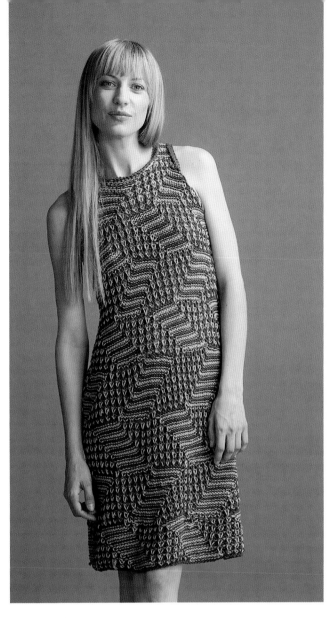

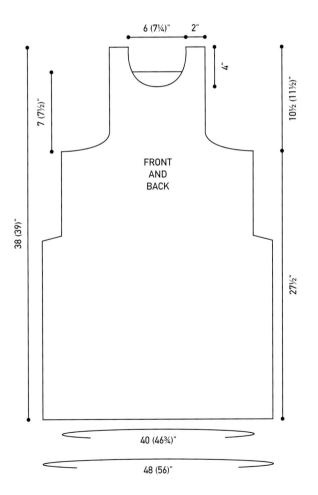

6 (7¼)" 2"

4"

7 (7½)"

10½ (11½)"

FRONT
AND
BACK

38 (39)"

27½"

40 (46¾)"

48 (56)"

FINISHING

Block lightly. Sew right shoulder seam.

Neckband: With RS facing, using smaller needle and A, beginning at left Front shoulder, pick up and knit 65 (75) sts along neck shaping. Begin St st, beginning with a purl row. Work even for 3 rows. Purl 1 row (turning row). Work even for 3 rows. BO all sts, working 1 st from live edge together with corresponding st from WS of pick-up edge as you BO. Sew left shoulder and Neckband seam.

Armhole Edging: With RS facing, using smaller needle and A, beginning at center underarm, pick up and knit 83 (88) sts around armhole edge. Begin St st, beginning with a purl row. Work even for 3 rows. Purl 1 row (turning row). Work even for 3 rows. BO as for Neckband. Sew seam.

folded mini dress

This dress will show off your curves, starting with a deeply textured skirt that seems to unfold above the hips into a fitted silhouette all the way to the shoulders. Because it is knit with Rowan's Felted Tweed, a lightweight yarn that can be worked on larger-than-recommended needles without becoming lacy, the dress feels almost weightless despite the additional fabric for the folds (worked in Folded Fabric [see page 75], modified for circular knitting). The dress is reversible not only by turning it inside out, but also by turning it front to back to change the depth of the vee (compare the photo at right with the photo on the right on page 120).

LYNNE BARR

SIZES

X-Small (Small, Medium, Large, X-Large, 2X-Large)
To fit bust sizes 28-30 (32-34, 36-38, 40-42, 46-48, 50-52)"
Shown in size X-Small

FINISHED MEASUREMENTS

28¾ (33½, 38½, 43¼, 48, 52¾)" chest
Note: This dress is meant to fit very close. If you prefer a less close fit, you may wish to work the next size larger.

YARN

Rowan Yarns Felted Tweed (50% merino wool / 25% alpaca / 25% viscose/rayon; 190 yards / 50 grams): 5 (6, 7, 8, 9, 10) balls #153 Phantom

NEEDLES

One 24" (60 cm) long or longer circular (circ) needle size US 8 (5 mm)
One 24" (60 cm) long or longer circular needle size US 7 (4.5 mm)
One double-pointed needle (dpn) size US 6 (4 mm) or smaller, to pick up sts in Folded Fabric
Change needle size if necessary to obtain correct gauge.

NOTIONS

Stitch markers; removable marker; stitch holders

GAUGE

20 sts and 28 rows = 4" (10 cm) in Stockinette stitch (St st), using size US 7 needle

NOTES

This pattern is worked in the rnd from the bottom edge to the armholes, then the Front and Back are worked separately back and forth to the end of the shoulders, which are grafted together. The Dress is reversible not only by turning it inside out, but also by turning it front to back. For the purposes of the instructions, the shallower vee will be in the Front, and the deeper vee will be in the Back, however, the dress can be worn either way.

STITCH PATTERN

FOLDED FABRIC
(multiple of 16 sts; 19-rnd repeat)
Note: This version of Folded Fabric is worked in K8, P8 rib, instead of the K6, P6 rib shown on page 75. It is also worked in the rnd, rather than back and forth.
Rnds 1-8: *K8, p8; repeat from * around.
Rnd 9: *Rotate work forward so opposite side is showing and knitting is above needle. Using dpn, pick up sts 5-8 of current repeat on opposite side of work, 7 rows below current row (see photo 1, page 75). Rotate work back and hold dpn behind and parallel to main needle (see photo 2, page 75) [K2tog (1 st on needle together with 1 st on dpn, see photo 2, page 75)] 4 times, k4, p8; repeat from * around.
Rnds 10-18: *K8, p8; repeat from * around.
Rnd 19: *K8, p4, using dpn, pick up sts 13-16 of current repeat on front side of work, 7 rows below current row, [p2tog (1 st from dpn with 1 st from needle)] 4 times; repeat from * around.
Repeat Rnds 1-19 for Folded Fabric.

DRESS

Using larger circ needle, CO 192 (224, 256, 288, 320, 352) sts. Join for working in the rnd, being careful not to twist sts; place marker (pm) for beginning of rnd. Begin Folded Fabric. Work even until 6 vertical repeats of the pattern have been completed. Work Rnd 1 once (piece should measure approximately 11" from the beginning). *Note: If you would like a longer skirt, you may work another vertical pattern repeat, which will add 2" in length.*

SKIRT

Shape Hip and Waist

Decrease Rnd 1: Change to smaller circ needle. *K2tog, k6, p8; repeat from * around—180 (210, 240, 270, 300, 330) sts remain. Work even for 5 rnds.

Decrease Rnd 2: *K2tog, k5, p8; repeat from * around—168 (196, 224, 252, 280, 308) sts remain.
Work even for 5 rnds.

Decrease Rnd 3: *K2tog, k4, p8; repeat from * around—156 (182, 208, 234, 260, 286) sts remain.
Work even for 5 rnds.

Decrease Rnd 4: *K2tog, k3, p8; repeat from * around—144 (168, 192, 216, 240, 264) sts remain.
Work even for 5 rnds.

Decrease Rnd 5: *K2tog, k2, p8; repeat from * around—132 (154, 176, 198, 220, 242) sts remain.
Work even for 1"; place removable marker to indicate waist.
Work even until piece measures 2" from waist marker.

Shape Bust

Increase Rnd 1: *K3, p1, M1-p, p7, k3, p8; repeat from * around—138 (161, 184, 207, 230, 253) sts.
Work even for 7 rnds.

Increase Rnd 2: *K3, p9, k3, p7, M1-p, p1; repeat from * around—144 (168, 192, 216, 240, 264) sts.
Work even until piece measures 5" from waist marker.

Next Rnd: Change to Rev St st (purl every rnd). Work even until piece measures 7½ (8, 8½, 9, 9½, 9½)" from waist marker.

Next Rnd: [K1, p1] 1 (2, 3, 4, 5, 6) time(s), k1, p30 (34, 38, 42, 46, 50), k1, p1, k1, pm for center, k1, p1, k1, p30 (34, 38, 42, 46, 50), k1, [p1, k1] 1 (2, 3, 4, 5, 6) time(s), pm for side, [k1, p1] 1 (2, 3, 4, 5, 6) time(s), k1, purl to last 3 (5, 7, 9, 11, 13) sts, k1, [p1, k1] 1 (2, 3, 4, 5, 6) time(s). Work even for 2 rnds. Transfer next 72 (84, 96, 108, 120, 132) sts to spare circ needle for Front and set aside.

BACK

Shape Armholes and Neck

Note: For the purposes of the instructions, the WS will be the knit side, and the RS will be the purl side. The Dress can be worn with either side showing. On WS rows, slip first purl st of row purlwise; on RS rows, slip first knit st of row knitwise. Armhole and Neck shaping are worked simultaneously; please read entire section through before beginning.

Row 1 (WS): Working back and forth on Back sts only, BO 0 (2, 4, 6, 8, 10) sts in pattern, p1 (0, 0, 0, 0, 0), k1, p1, ssk, knit to 3 sts before center marker, p1, k1, p1, remove marker; join a second ball of yarn, slip 1 purlwise, k1, p1 (0, 0, 0, 0, 0), knit to last 5 (7, 9, 11, 13, 15) sts, k2tog, p1, [k1, p1] 1 (2, 3, 4, 5, 6) time(s).

Row 2: Right Back: BO 0 (2, 4, 6, 8, 10) sts in pattern, k1, p1, k1, purl to last 3 sts, k1, p1, k1; Left Back: Slip 1 knitwise, p1, k1, purl to last 3 sts, k1, p1, k1—35 (39, 43, 47, 51, 55) sts remain each side.

Row 3: Decrease 1 st each armhole edge this row, every other row 2 (5, 6, 12, 15, 17) times, then every 4 rows 3 (3, 3, 0, 0, 0) times, as established, and AT THE SAME TIME, decrease 1 st at neck edge this row, then every 4 rows 9 (10, 11, 10, 11, 11) times, as follows: Left Neck Edge: Work to last 5 sts, k2tog, p1, k1, p1; Right Neck Edge: Slip 1 purlwise, k1, p1, ssk, work to end—19 (19, 21, 23, 23, 25) sts remain each side for shoulders. Work even until armhole measures 6½ (7, 7½, 7½, 8, 8)" from beginning of shaping, ending with a WS row.

Shape Shoulders

Right Shoulder

Row 1 (RS): Work even.

Rows 2 and 3: Slip 1 purlwise, k1, p1, k3 (3, 4, 4, 4, 5), w&t, work to end.

Rows 4 and 5: Slip 1 purlwise, k1, p1, k9 (9, 10, 12, 12, 13), hiding wrap, w&t, work to end.

Row 6: Work even, hiding remaining wrap. Place sts on holder for finishing.

Left Shoulder

Rows 1 (RS) and 2: Slip 1 knitwise, p1, k1, p3 (3, 4, 4, 4, 5), w&t, work to end.

Rows 3 and 4: Slip 1 knitwise, p1, k1, p9 (9, 10, 12, 12, 13) hiding wrap, w&t, work to end.

Row 5: Work even, hiding remaining wrap. Place sts on holder for finishing.

FRONT

Shape Armholes

Note: Armhole and Neck shaping are worked simultaneously; please read entire section through before beginning.

Row 1 (WS): Rejoin yarn to Front sts. BO 0 (2, 4, 6, 8, 10) sts in pattern, p1 (0, 0, 0, 0, 0), k1, p1, ssk, work to last 5 (7, 9, 11, 13, 15) sts, k2tog, work to end.

Row 2: BO 0 (2, 4, 6, 8, 10) sts in pattern, k1, p1, k1, work to end.

Row 3: Decrease 1 st each side this row, every other row 3 (6, 7, 12, 15, 17) times, then every 4 rows 2 (2, 2, 0, 0, 0) times, as follows: Slip 1 purlwise, k1, p1, ssk, knit to last 5 sts, k2tog, p1, k1, p1, and AT THE SAME TIME, when armhole measures 2¾ (3¼, 3¾, 3¾, 4¼, 4¼)" from beginning of shaping, ending with a RS row, begin neck shaping.

Shape Neck

Setup Row (WS): Place marker between 2 center sts. Continuing armhole shaping as established, work to 3 sts before center marker, p1, k1, p1, slip marker (sm), p1, k1, p1, work to end. Work even for 1 row.

Decrease Row (WS): Continuing armhole shaping, work to 5 sts before center marker, k2tog, p1, k1, p1, remove marker; join a second ball of yarn, slip 1 purlwise, k1, p1, ssk, work to end. Working both sides at same time, work even for 1 row.

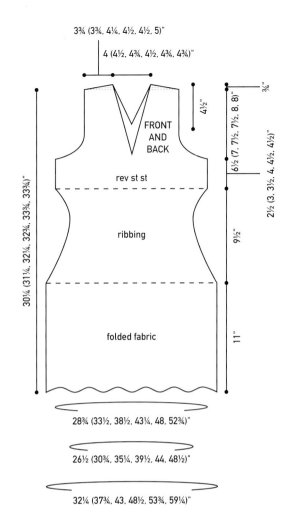

3¾ (3¾, 4¼, 4½, 4½, 5)"

4 (4½, 4¾, 4½, 4¾, 4¾)"

FRONT AND BACK

rev st st

ribbing

folded fabric

4½"

¾"

6½ (7, 7½, 7½, 8, 8)"

2½ (3, 3½, 4, 4½, 4½)"

9½"

11"

30¼ (31¼, 32¼, 32¾, 33¾, 33¾)"

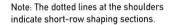

28¾ (33½, 38½, 43¼, 48, 52¾)"

26½ (30¾, 35¼, 39½, 44, 48½)"

32¼ (37¾, 43, 48½, 53¾, 59¼)"

Note: The dotted lines at the shoulders indicate short-row shaping sections.

Next Row (WS): Continuing armhole shaping, decrease 1 st each neck edge this row, every other row 7 (8, 10, 9, 10, 10) times, then every 4 rows 1 (1, 0, 0, 0, 0) time(s), as follows: Right Neck Edge: Work to last 5 sts, k2tog, p1, k1, p1; Left Neck Edge: Slip 1 purlwise, k1, p1, ssk, work to end–19 (19, 21, 23, 23, 25) sts remain each side for shoulders after all shaping is complete. Work even until armhole measures 6½ (7, 7½, 7½, 8, 8)" from beginning of shaping, ending with a WS row. Shape shoulders as for Front.

FINISHING

Graft shoulder sts together using Kitchener st (see page 183).

double-wrap stockings

Feeling a little naughty but nice? Without abandoning good taste, Debbie has found a way to spice up your look. She has cleverly worked up a long and shapely pair of stockings by combining short rows with her reversible "double-wrap bind-off stitch," to produce a fancier, more feminine alternative to the common fishnet style.

DEBBIE NEW

SIZES
One size
Note: These Stockings are extremely stretchy because of the stitch pattern and the elastic content of the yarn used, and should fit a very wide range of sizes. If you would like to make the Stockings wider, the instructions indicate where to do so.

FINISHED MEASUREMENTS
7" from toe to back of heel, unstretched
20½" from back of heel to top of leg, unstretched
9" circumference at top of leg, unstretched

YARN
Knit One Crochet Two Soxx Appeal (96% superwash merino wool / 3% nylon / 1% elastic; 208 yards / 50 grams): 3 balls #9692 Marine Blue

NEEDLES
Two 32" (80 cm) long or longer circular (circ) needles size US 11 (8 mm)
One 32" (80 cm) long or longer circular needle size US 15 (10 mm)
One double-pointed needle (dpn) size US 10 (6 mm) or smaller, for picking up sts
Change needle size if necessary to obtain correct gauge.

NOTIONS
Waste yarn; stitch markers

GAUGE
20 sts = 4" (10 cm) in double-wrap BO stitch, unstretched, using smaller needles.
Note: Twenty sts of double-wrap BO stitch will yield 48 to 48½" of yarn, unraveled and stretched to its fullest extent.

ABBREVIATIONS
K1-tbl-wy2: Knit 1 st through back, wrapping yarn twice.
Dwb (double-wrap BO): K1-tbl-wy2, pass a single wrap from the previous st (the wrap that is easiest to pick up from the front) over the 2 wraps of the last st worked. *Note: Where there is a marker between the st just worked and the wrap that is to be passed over, pass the wrap over the marker as well.*
Dw2tog: K2tog-tbl, wrapping yarn twice, pass a single wrap from the previous st (the wrap that is easiest to pick up from the front) over the 2 wraps of the last st worked.
Pwo (pass wrap over): Pass a single wrap from the previous st (the wrap that is easiest to pick up from the front) over the last st worked.
Bhw (BO half wrap): Pass the second wrap of the last st on the needle over its own first wrap. *Note: This is worked only at the end of the row, after the last st has been worked k1-tbl-wy2.*

TIPS

Make sure that only 1 wrap is lifted over each time you work dwb, and that it lifts over 3 strands, the two wraps of the first stitch on the needle and the remaining wrap of the second stitch. Pulling down on the knit fabric helps to identify the correct thread if in doubt.

Since double-wrap stitches are bound-off as you work, mistakes can only be corrected by unpicking your work, so check every ten or fifteen stitches to make sure that your stitches were worked correctly. Each stitch should slightly cross over the neighboring stitches to either side of it. If you have to unpick your work, untwist the last stitch by two half twists, then lift the back of the stitch and hook the needle into it again.

STOCKINGS

Note: Stockings are worked in two halves that are joined at the center by the Provisional CO. Each half is worked from center top edge, down front of leg to toe, along underside of foot to heel, then up back of calf to top. The front and back of each half are then joined by a zip st after both halves are complete.

Using larger circ needle, waste yarn, and Provisional CO (see page 178), CO 278 sts.

FIRST SIDE

Set-Up Row: Change to working yarn. K135 for front, place marker (pm) for toe, k36 for foot, pm for heel, k26 for back, *pm for short-row shaping, k27; repeat from * twice. Transfer sts and markers to smaller circ needle, making sure not to twist sts.

Shape Leg

Note: Leg is shaped in 3 segments. Within each segment, Increase Rows A, B, and C are each worked once.

Increase Row A: K1-tbl-wy2, *dwb; repeat from * to 8 sts before first marker, k1-tbl, pwo, [k1, pso] 7 times, slip marker (sm), yf, slip 1 st, yb, pass last BO st (before marker) over marker and last st worked, slip 1 st, yf, slip both slipped sts back to left-hand needle, turn.

Increase Row B: With dpn, pick up 8 sts from BO sts, sm, k2, [k1, pso] 3 times, k1-wy2, pass second st on right-hand needle over 2 wraps of last st, *dwb; repeat from * to end, bhw.

Increase Row C: K1-tbl-wy2, *dwb; repeat from * to BO sts before marker; with dpn, pick up 4 sts from BO sts, removing marker, [dwb] 4 times, [dw2tog] twice (loop behind next st together with next st on left-hand needle; do not turn.

Repeat Increase Rows A-C twice, omitting first k1-tbl-wy2 on Row A, and ending 2 sts before heel marker. *Dwb; repeat from * to end, bhw.

Straight Row: K1-tbl-wy2, *dwb; repeat from * to end, bhw.

Decrease Row: K1-tbl-wy2, [*dwb; repeat from * to 4 sts before next marker, [dw2tog] twice, sm, [dw2tog] twice] twice, *dwb; repeat from * to end–270 sts remain.

Repeat Decrease Row once–262 sts remain (131 sts on either side of toe marker). Break yarn. Leave sts on needle for zipping.

SECOND SIDE

With Provisional CO at the top and purl bumps in waste yarn facing you, insert smaller circ needle into each purl bump from back to front. You should have the same number of sts as CO for First Side; pick up an extra st at one end of row if necessary. Remove waste yarn. Make sure all sts are oriented on the needle as for normal knit sts, with none twisted. Place markers as for First Side. Work as for First Side, beginning with Shape Leg.

TO WORK LARGER SIZES

Before zipping up the sides, make sure Stocking will fit comfortably. To add 1" to the circumference, work 1 additional Decrease Row on each side before zipping up the sides. Note that you will end at the cuff instead of at the toe, so you will have to zip up the sides from the cuff to the toe.

To add 2" to the circumference, work 1 additional Straight Row on each side before zipping up the sides.

ZIPPING UP SIDES

Holding needle so that yarn is at right-hand end of needle, slip all sts purlwise before toe marker to right-hand needle, removing marker and being careful not to untwist any sts; turn. *Note: Zipping alternates working on the right-hand needle with working on the left-hand needle; be sure you are alternating needles and not untwisting sts.* Slip 2 sts purlwise to right-hand needle, pass 2 sts over them; slip 3 sts purlwise to left-hand needle, pass 2 sts over the first st; *slip 2 sts purlwise to right-hand needle, pass second st over first st; slip 2 sts to left-hand needle, pass second st over first; repeat from * until 1 st remains. Fasten off.

FINISHING

You will have a few ends to sew in and that's it. Except, of course, there is that troubling matter of the second Stocking.

winding path

WENLAN CHIA

This bold and playful pullover can be worn as a short Empire style with an abundantly sized white cowl collar (shown at right), or it can be turned upside down to wear as a longer tunic with a grey and black striped turtleneck (see page 129). Or it can be worn inside out in either style. Wenlan's plush, chunky yarn is deceptively lightweight. It knits into a highly defined rib with a three-dimensional feel that would be unattainable with a fine-gauge yarn.

SIZES

Small (Medium, Large, X-Large)
Shown in size Small

FINISHED MEASUREMENTS

29 (32, 35, 37¾)" chest, stretched

YARN

Twinkle Yarns Soft Chunky (100% wool; 83 yards / 200 grams): 4 (4, 5, 6) hanks #51 Hazel (MC); 1 hank each #08 White (A) and #09 Black (B)

NEEDLES

One 24" (60 cm) long or longer circular (circ) needle size US 19 (15 mm)
Change needle size if necessary to obtain correct gauge.

NOTIONS

Stitch markers; stitch holder

GAUGE

6 sts and 9½ rows = 4" (10 cm) in Stockinette stitch (St st)
5½ sts and 9½ rows = 4" in K2, P2 Rib, stretched

STITCH PATTERNS

K2, P2 RIB IN-THE-RND
(multiple of 4 sts; 1-rnd repeat)
All Rnds: *K2, p2; repeat from * to end.

K2, P2 RIB
(multiple of 4 sts + 1; 2-row repeat)
Row 1 (RS): *K2, p2; repeat from * to last st, k1.
Row 2: P1, *k2, p2; repeat from * to end.
Repeat Rows 1 and 2 for K2, P2 Rib.

ABBREVIATIONS

LI (lifted increase): Knit into st below next st on left-hand needle.
LI2-p (doubled purled lifted increase): Working from back to front, with left-hand needle, lift loop of st below last st on right-hand needle, purl into back, then front of this loop.

NOTES

The pullover is totally reversible, both inside-out and upside-down. However, for the purposes of the instructions, one side will be labeled RS and the other side WS. The Neck in the instructions will become the Body, and vice versa, when worn upside down.

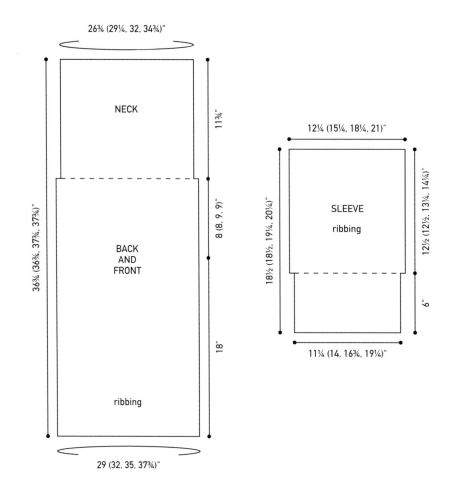

26¾ (29¼, 32, 34¾)"

NECK

11¾"

36¾ (36¾, 37¾, 37¾)"

BACK
AND
FRONT

8 (8, 9, 9)"

18"

ribbing

29 (32, 35, 37¾)"

12¼ (15¼, 18¼, 21)"

SLEEVE
ribbing

12½ (12½, 13¼, 14¼)"

18½ (18½, 19¼, 20¼)"

6"

11¼ (14, 16¾, 19¼)"

NOTE: All ribbing measurements are stretched.

BODY

Using A, CO 40 (44, 48, 52) sts. Join for working in the rnd, being careful not to twist sts; place marker (pm) for beginning of rnd. Begin K2, P2 Rib in-the-Rnd. Work even for 5 rnds. Pm after st 17.

Shape Ribbing

Shaping Rnd 1: Work to 3 sts before marker, k3tog, work 21 (21, 25, 25) sts, M1-r, LI, work to end.
Work even for 4 rnds, knitting the increased sts.
Next Rnd: Change to MC. Work even for 2 rnds.
Shaping Rnd 2: Work to 3 sts before marker, k3tog, work 21 (21, 25, 25) sts, LI2-p, work to end. Work even for 6 rnds, purling the increased sts.
Next Rnd: *Repeat Shaping Rnd 1. Work even for 5 rnds. Repeat Shaping Rnd 2. Work even for 5 rnds. Repeat from * once, removing second marker after last repeat. Work even until piece measures 18" from the beginning.

BACK

Shape Armhole: Work 20 (22, 24, 26) sts, transfer to st holder for Front, work to end. Working back and forth on remaining 20 (22, 24, 26) sts, work even until armhole measures 8 (8, 9, 9)" from split, ending with a WS row. Transfer sts to st holder.

FRONT

Shape Armhole: With WS facing, rejoin yarn to sts on holder. Complete as for Back.

NECK

Work across Front sts, then Back sts from holder—40 (44, 48, 52) sts. Join for working in the rnd; pm for beginning of rnd.
Next Rnd: Change to St st. Work even for 16 rnds. Change to B; work even for 4 rnds. Change to MC; work even for 4 rnds. Change to B; work even for 4 rnds. BO all sts.

SLEEVES

Using MC, CO 17 (21, 25, 29) sts; begin St st. Work even for 14 rows.
Next Row (RS): Change to K2, P2 Rib. Work even until piece measures 18½ (18½, 19¼, 20¼)" from the beginning, ending with a WS row. BO all sts in pattern.

FINISHING

Sew in Sleeves. Sew Sleeve seams.

faux wrap

Chic and well behaved, Lily's Faux Wrap pullover utilizes classic styling rather than radical shape to provide a flattering elegance. The modern fitted silhouette, that hugs you in just the right places, is tied with I-cord and neatly wraps up the look. Lily's signature reversible cables, used on both collar and cuffs, allow the collar to be worn buttoned up or opened, and the sleeves to be worn either full length or folded back for a three-quarter length.

SIZES

X-Small (Small, Medium, Large, X-Large)
Shown in size Small

FINISHED MEASUREMENTS

34½ (37, 41, 44, 46½)" chest

YARN

Lily Chin Signature Collection Park Avenue (60% merino wool / 40% alpaca; 109 yards / 50 grams): 9 (10, 11, 13, 14) balls #04 Dove Gray

NEEDLES

One pair straight needles size US 8 (5 mm)
One pair double-pointed needles (dpn) size US 8 (5 mm)
Change needle size if necessary to obtain correct gauge.

NOTIONS

Cable needle (cn); stitch marker; one ⅝" button

GAUGE

17 sts and 23 rows = 4" (10 cm) in Stockinette stitch (St st)
28 sts = 3¼" over cable pattern from Chart A

NOTES

The Cable Panel for each piece is worked first, then the sts for that piece are picked up from the side edge of the Cable panel, and worked up. The Cable Panels are completely reversible. However, for the purposes of the instructions, each Cable Panel will have a RS and a WS.

BACK CABLE PANEL

CO 28 sts very tightly; begin Chart A, beginning on Row 15 (1, 15, 1, 15) of Chart. Work even until piece measures 18 (19½, 21, 22½, 24)" from the beginning, ending with Row 13 (9, 13, 9, 13). BO all sts very tightly in pattern. Do not break yarn.

BACK

With RS of Back Cable Panel facing, rotate piece 90 degrees, pick up and knit 77 (83, 91, 97, 103) sts evenly spaced along left side edge of Panel. Begin St st, beginning with a purl row.

Shape Waist (RS): Decrease 1 st each side this row, [every 4 rows, then every other row] twice, then every 4 rows once, as follows: K2, k2tog, work to last 4 sts, ssk, k2—65 (71, 79, 85, 91) sts remain. Work even until piece measures 7½" from the beginning, including Back Cable Panel, ending with a WS row.

Shape Bust (RS): Increase 1 st each side this row, then every 6 rows 3 times, as follows: K2, M1, work to last 2 sts, M1-r, k2—73 (79, 87, 93, 99) sts. Work even until piece measures 13½ (13½, 14, 14, 14½)" from the beginning, including Back Cable Panel, ending with a WS row.

Shape Armholes (RS): BO 5 (5, 6, 6, 7) sts at beginning of next 2 rows, then decrease 1 st each side every other row 4 (4, 5, 6, 6) times, as follows: K2, k2tog, work to last 4 sts, ssk, k2—55 (61, 65, 69, 73) sts remain. Work even until armhole measures 8 (8½, 8½, 9, 9)" from beginning of shaping, ending with a WS row.

Shape Shoulders and Back Neck (RS): BO 4 (4, 5, 5, 5) sts, work 12 (14, 14, 15, 16) sts, join a second ball of yarn and BO center 23 (25, 27, 29, 31) sts, work to end. Working both sides at the same time, BO 4 (4, 5, 5, 5) sts at beginning of next row, 3 (4, 4, 4, 4) sts at beginning of next 2 rows, 3 (4, 4, 4, 5) sts at beginning of next 2 rows, then 4 (4, 4, 5, 5) sts at beginning of next 2 rows, and AT THE SAME TIME, decrease 1 st at each neck edge twice.

FRONT CABLE PANEL

Work as for Back Cable Panel, beginning on Row 15 (11, 15, 11, 15) of Chart, and ending on Row 13 (19, 13, 19, 13).

FRONT

Work as for Back until armholes measure 4 (4¼, 4, 4, 3¾)" from beginning of shaping, ending with a WS row.

Shape Neck (RS): Place marker before center st. Continuing armhole shaping, work across to marker, join a separate ball of yarn, BO center st, work to end. Working both sides at the same time, work even for 1 row.

Next Row (RS): Decrease 1 st at each neck edge this row, then every other row 12 (13, 14, 15, 16) times, as follows: On left neck edge, work to last 4 sts, ssk, k2; on right neck edge, k2, k2tog, work to end. AT THE SAME TIME, when armholes measure same as for Back to shoulder shaping, shape shoulders as for Back.

SLEEVE CABLE PANEL

CO 28 sts very tightly; begin Chart A, beginning on Row 15 (15, 11, 11, 7) of Chart. Work even until piece measures 9½ (9½, 10¾, 10¾, 12)" from the beginning, ending with Row 15 (15, 19, 19, 3) of Chart. BO all sts very tightly in pattern. Do not break yarn.

SLEEVES

With RS of Sleeve Cable Panel facing, rotate piece 90 degrees, pick up and knit 41 (41, 47, 47, 51) sts evenly spaced along left side edge of Panel. Begin St st, beginning with a purl row.

Shape Sleeve (RS): Increase 1 st each side this row, every 8 (6, 6, 4, 4) rows 5 (7, 4, 3, 4) times, then every 10 (8, 8, 6, 6) rows 2 (2, 4, 7, 6) times, as follows: K2, M1, work to last 2 sts, M1-r, k2—57 (61, 65, 69, 73) sts. Work even until piece measures 15¾ (15¼, 14¾, 14¼, 13¾)" from the beginning, including Sleeve Cable Panel, ending with a WS row.

Shape Cap (RS): BO 5 (5, 6, 6, 7) sts at beginning of next 2 rows, then decrease 1 st each side every other row 12 (13, 14, 15, 16) times, as follows: K2, k2tog, work to last 4 sts, ssk, k2. BO 3 sts at beginning of next 4 rows. BO remaining 11 (13, 13, 15, 15) sts.

KEY

☐ Knit on RS, purl on WS.

⊡ Purl on RS, knit on WS.

⩔ Slip st purlwise.

Slip 4 sts to cn, hold to front, [k1, p1]
twice, [k1, p1] twice from cn.

CHART A

Back, Front, and Sleeve Cable Panels

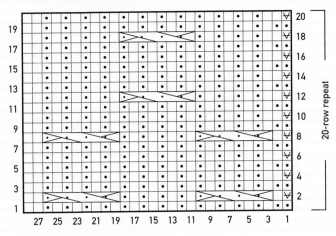

CHART B

Collar Cable Panel

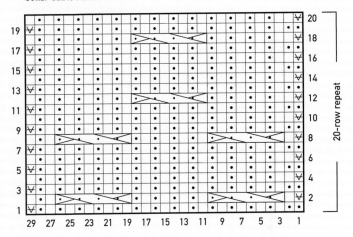

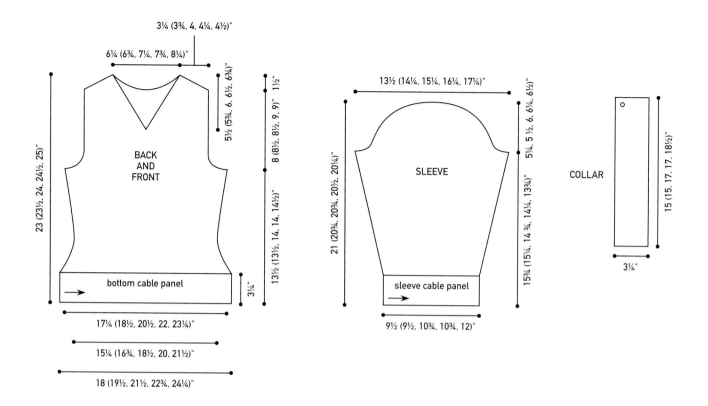

COLLAR

CO 29 sts very tightly; begin Chart B, beginning on Row 7 (7, 1, 1, 15) of Chart. Work even until piece measures 14½ (14½, 16½, 16½, 18)" from the beginning, ending with a WS row.

Buttonhole Row (RS): Work to last 8 sts, k2tog, yo, work to end. Work even until piece measures 15 (15, 17, 17, 18½)" from the beginning, ending with Row 3 (3, 9, 9, 13) of Chart. BO all sts very tightly in pattern.

FINISHING

Block pieces to measurements. Sew shoulder seams. Set in Sleeves; sew side and Sleeve seams. *Note: To make the Sleeve Cable Panels reversible, and make the edge tighter, rather than sewing the Sleeve Cable Panel edges together, use Kitchener st (see page 183) and graft only the knit sts on the RS.*

With RS of garment and Collar facing, sew Garter st side edge of Collar to neck shaping, beginning and ending 2 (2½, 2½, 3, 3)" above base of neck. *Note: Buttonhole should be on right side of neck. Sew button opposite buttonhole.*

I-Cord Ties: Using dpn, CO 3 sts; *transfer needle with sts to left hand, bring yarn around behind work to right-hand side; using second dpn, knit sts from right to left, pulling yarn from left to right for first st; do not turn. Slide sts to opposite end of needle; repeat from * until piece measures 24 (30, 36, 42, 48)" long. Fasten off. Work a second I-Cord 81 (90, 99, 108, 117)" long. Attach shorter I-Cord to left side seam at last increase. Attach longer I-Cord to base of neck.

syncopation

From the tips of its sporty striped ties to the geometric motif
at its center, Nancy's headband is the perfect little project packed
with techniques to expand your brioche skills. Using syncopation,
a technique that switches knit and purl columns to change the
foreground color, along with increases and decreases specific
to brioche, the headband can be worked in the lightweight
all-season yarn shown here, or with a heavier yarn for a stylish
way to keep one's ears warm in cold weather.

FINISHED MEASUREMENTS

2¾" wide x 18" long, not including Ties

YARN

Zitron Trekking Pro Natura (75% wool / 25% bamboo;
459 yards / 100 grams): 1 skein each #1506 Pine (DC)
and #1535 Cream (LC)

NEEDLES

One pair double-pointed needles (dpn) size US 0 (2 mm)
Change needle size if necessary to obtain correct gauge.

NOTIONS

Cable needle (cn)

GAUGE

15 sts and 20 counted rows (40 worked rows) = 2" (5 cm)
in Two-Color Brioche
Note: See notes in pattern for information on counting sts and rows.

ABBREVIATIONS

Note: All slipped stitches are slipped purlwise.
DS (dark side of work): The knit columns on this side are
worked in the dark color.
LS (light side of work): The knit columns on this side are
worked in the light color.
DC: Dark color
LC: Light color

NANCY MARCHANT

Brk (brioche knit, also known as bark): Knit the st (that was slipped in the row before) together with its yo.

Brp (brioche purl, also known as burp): Purl the st (that was slipped in the row before) together with its yo.

Yfsl1yo: Bring yarn under needle to front of work, slip following st purlwise, then bring yarn over needle (and over slipped st) to back of work.

Yfsl2yo: Same as yfsl1yo, but 2 sts are slipped, instead of 1.

Sl1yo: With yarn already in front, slip 1 st purlwise, then bring yarn over needle (and over slipped st) to back of work.

Sl1yof: Leaving yarn in front, slip following st purlwise. Bring yarn over needle (and over slipped st), and then under needle to front.

Yf: Bring yarn to front, under needle.

Yb: Bring yarn to back, under needle.

Inc1r (increase 1 st right-slanting): With left-hand needle, pick up 1 st 2 rows below st just worked in last knit column and knit it.

Inc1l (increase 1 st left-slanting): With right-hand needle, pick up 1 st 1 row below next knit st on left-hand needle, place it on left-hand needle and knit it. *Note: If the next knit st is the second st on left-hand needle, skip over the first st to reach the next knit column, pick up the st as indicated and place it on left-hand needle in front of skipped st.*

T1lyo2 (twist st left in preparation for left-slanting decrease): Slip next st to cn, hold to front, slip 1, slip st from cn back to left-hand needle. *Note: when you work the next st, you will yo the 2 slipped sts on right-hand needle.*

T1ryo (twist st right in preparation for right-slanting decrease): With yarn in front, slip next st, slip following st to cn, hold to back, transfer first slipped st back to left-hand needle.

Brssk (slip, slip, bark slipped sts tog; 1-st left-slanting decrease): There are 2 ways to work brssk. 1) Slip next 2 sts to right-hand needle 1 at a time as if to knit, insert point of left-hand needle from behind into the 2 slipped sts, knit them together. *Note: Since a st and its yo are considered 1 st, this may mean that you slip 3 loops (2 sts and a yo), 1 at a time, onto the right-hand needle.* 2) If you have 2 sts hanging under 1 yo, go under yo, slip 2 sts to right-hand needle 1 at a time as if to knit, insert point of left-hand needle from behind into the 2 slipped sts, knit them together, allowing yo to slip off needle after working sts together.

Brk2tog (bark 2 sts together; 1-st right-slanting decrease): There are 2 ways to work brk2tog. 1) Knit next 2 sts together. *Note: Since a st and its yo are considered 1 st, this could mean that you have 3 loops (2 sts and a yo) hanging on the needle; knit them together.* 2) If you have 2 sts hanging under 1 yo, go under yo and knit the 2 sts together, allowing yo to slip off needle after working sts together.

STITCH PATTERNS

STRIPED RIB

(odd number of sts; 4-row repeat)

Note: The letters after the Row number indicate which color you are to use to work the row.

Set-Up Row: Join LC. K1, *p1, k1; repeat from * to end; turn.

Row 1 DC: Hold LC to back, bring DC from underneath LC, p1, *k1, p1; repeat from * to end. Do not turn; slide sts to opposite end of needle (hereafter, "slide").

Row 2 LC: P1, *k1, p1; repeat from * to end; turn.

Row 3 DC: Hold LC to back, bring DC from underneath LC, k1, *p1, k1; repeat from * to end. Do not turn; slide.

Row 4 LC: K1, *p1, k1; repeat from * to end; turn.

Repeat Rows 1-4 for Striped Rib Pattern.

TWO-COLOR BRIOCHE

(odd number of sts; 2-row repeat, counted rows [4 worked rows])

Set-Up Row DC: K1, *yfsl1yo, k1; repeat from * to end. Do not turn; slide sts to opposite end of needle (hereafter, "slide").

Set-Up Row LC: With LC in back, slip 1, yf, *brp1, sl1yof; repeat from * to last 2 sts, brp1, yb, slip 1; turn.

Row 1 LS DC: Bring LC to front, hold LC across front of first st, then with DC, p1 (this will catch the LC to make a nice selvage), *sl1yof, brp1; repeat from * to last 2 sts, sl1yof, p1. Do not turn; slide.

Row 1 LS LC: With LC in front, slip 1, yb, *brk1, yfsl1yo; repeat from * to last 2 sts, brk1, yf, slip 1; turn.

Row 2 DS DC: Bring LC to front, bring DC from underneath LC, k1 (this will catch the LC to make a nice selvage), *yfsl1yo, brk1; repeat from * to last 2 sts, yfsl1yo, k1. Do not turn; slide.

Row 2 DS LC: With LC in back, slip 1, yf, *brp1, sl1yof; repeat from * to last 2 sts, brp1, yb, slip 1; turn.

Repeat Rows 1 and 2, DC and LC, for Two-Color Brioche.

NOTES

The Headband is worked in Two-Color Brioche Stitch and is reversible. This means that there is no RS and WS; instead, there is a dark side (DS) and a light side (LS). The dark side uses the dark color (DC) in its knit columns and the light color (LC) in its purl columns. On the light side, the reverse is true; the light color creates the knit columns and the dark color creates the purl columns. Each row is worked twice, once with the dark color and once with the light color.

Each row is denoted first by the dominant color of the side, then by the particular color you are to use for that row. Therefore, if you are working a "DS LC" row, you are on the dark side, with the dominant dark columns facing you, and you will be working the receding light columns with the light colored yarn. You only count the knit column stitches on one side when counting rows. If you are told to work 8 counted rows, you will work until there are 8 knit column stitches on the side facing you. This equals 16 worked rows, since you actually work each row twice, once in each color. The easiest way to count knit column stitches is to count in the knit column next to the selvage stitch. When making increase rows, it can be difficult to determine when to increase, but if you count the light side light color (LS LC) knit column at the edge and mark rows, you should be able to keep your count.

Remember that a stitch with its yarnover is considered 1 stitch when counting. The yarnover never counts as a st. In this pattern, you will read "work to last 4 sts". You will actually have 6 loops hanging on the left-hand needle but you will count 4 stitches because 2 of the loops are yarnovers over a stitch, and you count them together as 1 stitch. Also brk2tog means that you knit 2 entire stitches (sometimes 3 loops hanging on the needle) together.

When working increases and decreases in brioche knitting, you need to increase and decrease 2 stitches at one time in order to maintain the pattern. For this Headband, you will increase and decrease 1 stitch on the light side and then 1 stitch on the dark side for each set of increases or decreases. When working increases, you will be asked to skip over a stitch and pick up stitches in the knit columns in the rows below. When working decreases, you will be asked to rearrange the stitches so that, for example, 2 light column stitches are next to each other to work them together for a decrease. This may seem tedious when you are working, but it is what allows the piece to be reversible.

The motif in the center of the Headband is worked in Syncopated Brioche. To work Syncopated Brioche, you reverse knit and purl columns, so that when working the pattern in 2 colors, the former dominant columns will now be worked in purl, making them recede, and the former receding columns will be worked in knit, making them dominant.

These instructions include the yarn manipulation necessary to make an attractive selvedge edge. This edge is not worked later in finishing, so it needs to be handled while knitting it.

HEADBAND

Note: All slipped stitches are slipped purlwise.

FIRST TIE

Using DC, CO 9 sts. Do not turn; slide sts to opposite end of needle. Begin Striped Rib. Work even until piece measures 6" from the beginning, ending with Row 2; turn.

Next Row: Change to Two-Color Brioche. Work even until you have 8 counted LC rows on LS (16 worked rows), and are ready to work Row 1 LS LC.

SHAPE HEADBAND

Increase Row 1 LS LC: With LC in front, slip 1, yb, brk1, yfsl1yo, brk1, inc1r, yfsl1yo, inc1l, brk1, yfsl1yo, brk1, yf, slip 1–11 sts. Turn work.

Increase Row 1 DS DC: Bring LC to front, bring DC from underneath LC and k1, yfsl1yo, brk1, yfsl1yo, inc1r, yfsl1yo, brk1, yfsl1yo, inc1l, yfsl1yo, brk1, yfsl1yo, k1–13 sts. Do not turn; slide. Work even until you have 16 counted LC rows (32 worked rows), ending with Row 1 LS DC.

Increase Row 2 LS LC: With LC in front, slip 1, yb, brk1, yfsl1yo, brk1, inc1r, work to last 4 sts, inc1l, brk1, yfsl1yo, brk1, yf, slip 1–15 sts. Turn work.

Increase Row 2 DS DC: Bring LC to front, bring DC from underneath LC and k1, yfsl1yo, brk1, yfsl1yo, inc1r, *yfsl1yo, brk1; repeat from * to last 5 sts, yfsl1yo, inc1l, yfsl1yo, brk1, yfsl1yo, k1–17 sts. Do not turn; slide. Work even until you have 24 counted LC rows (48 worked rows), ending with Row 1 LSDC.

Repeat Increase Rows 3 and 4 once–21 sts. Work even until you have 44 counted LC rows (88 working rows), ending with Row 1 LS LC. Piece should measure approximately 6" from end of Tie.

WORK MOTIF
Begin Syncopated Brioche
Syncopated Row 1 DS DC: Bring LC to front, bring DC from underneath LC and k1, [yfsl1yo, brk1] 4 times, yf, sl1yof, brp1, sl1yo, brk1, [yfsl1yo, brk1] 3 times, yfsl1yo, k1. Do not turn; slide.
Syncopated Row 1 DS LC: With LC in back, slip 1, yf, [brp1, sl1yof] 3 times, brp1, sl1yo, brk1, yfsl1yo, brk1, yf, [sl1yof, brp1] 4 times, yb, slip 1; turn.
Syncopated Row 2 LS DC: Hold LC across front of first st, then with DC, p1, [sl1yof, brp1] 4 times, sl1yo, brk1, yf, [sl1yof, brp1] 3 times, sl1yof, p1. Do not turn; slide.
Syncopated Row 2 LS LC: With LC in front, slip 1, yb, [brk1, yfsl1yo] 4 times, yf, brp1, sl1yof, brp1, sl1yo, brk1, [yfsl1yo, brk1] 3 times, yf, slip 1; turn.
Repeat Syncopated Rows 1 and 2, DC and LC, once.
Syncopated Row 3 DS DC: Bring LC to front, bring DC from underneath LC and k1, [yfsl1yo, brk1] 3 times, yf, [sl1yof, brp1] 3 times, [yfsl1yo, brk1] 3 times, yfsl1yo, k1. Do not turn; slide.
Syncopated Row 3 DS LC: With LC in back, slip 1, yf, [brp1, sl1yof] twice, brp1, sl1yo, [brk1, yfsl1yo] 3 times, brk1, yf, [sl1yof, brp1] 3 times, yb, slip 1; turn.
Syncopated Row 4 LS DC: Hold LC across front of first st, then with DC, p1, [sl1yof, brp1] 3 times, sl1yo, [brk1, yfsl1yo] 3 times, yf, [brp1, sl1yof] 3 times, p1. Do not turn; slide.
Syncopated Row 4 LS LC: With LC in front, slip 1, yb, [brk1, yfsl1yo] 3 times, yf, [brp1, sl1yof] 3 times, brp1, sl1yo, brk1, [yfsl1yo, brk1] twice, yf, slip 1; turn.
Repeat Syncopated Rows 3 and 4, DC and LC, once.
Syncopated Row 5 DS DC: Bring LC to front, bring DC from underneath LC and k1, [yfsl1yo, brk1] twice, yf, [sl1yof, brp1] 5 times, sl1yo, brk1, yfsl1yo, brk1, yfsl1yo, k1. Do not turn; slide.
Syncopated Row 5 DS LC: With LC in back, slip 1, yf, brp1, sl1yof, brp1, sl1yo, [brk1, yfsl1yo] 5 times, brk1, yf, [sl1yof, brp1] twice, yb, slip 1; turn.

Syncopated Row 6 LS DC: Hold LC across front of first st, then with DC, p1, [sl1yof, brp1] twice, sl1yo, [brk1, yfsl1yo] 5 times, yf, [brp1, sl1yof] twice, p1. Do not turn; slide.

Syncopated Row 6 LS LC: With LC in front, slip 1, yb, [brk1, yfsl1yo] twice, yf, [brp1, sl1yof] 5 times, brp1, sl1yo, brk1, yfsl1yo, brk1, yf, slip 1; turn.

Repeat Syncopated Rows 5 and 6, DC and LC, once.

Syncopated Row 7 DS DC: Bring LC to front, bring DC from underneath LC and k1, yfsl1yo, brk1, yf, [sl1yof, brp1] 3 times, sl1yo, brk1, yf, [sl1yof, brp1] 3 times, sl1yo, brk1, yfsl1yo, k1. Do not turn; slide.

Syncopated Row 7 DS LC: With LC in back, slip 1, yf, brp1, sl1yo, [brk1, yfsl1yo] 3 times, yf, brp1, sl1yof, brp1, sl1yo, [brk1, yfsl1yo] twice, brk1, yfsl1yof, brp1, yb, slip 1; turn.

Syncopated Row 8 LS DC: Hold LC across front of first st, then with DC, p1, sl1yof, brp1, sl1yo, [brk1, yfsl1yo] 3 times, yf, brp1, sl1yo, [brk1, yfsl1yo] twice, brk1, yf, sl1yof, brp1, sl1yof, p1. Do not turn; slide.

Syncopated Row 8 LS LC: With LC in front, slip 1, yb, brk1, yf, [sl1yof, brp1] 3 times, sl1yo, brk1, yfsl1yo, brk1, yf, [sl1yof, brp1] 3 times, sl1yo, brk1, yf, slip 1; turn.

Repeat Syncopated Rows 7 and 8, DC and LC, once.

Syncopated Row 9 DS DC: Bring LC to front, bring DC from underneath LC and k1, yf, [sl1yof, brp1] 3 times, sl1yo, [brk1, yfsl1yo] twice, brk1, yf, [sl1yof, brp1] 3 times, sl1yo, k1. Do not turn; slide.

Syncopated Row 9 DS LC: With LC in back, slip 1, [brk1, yfsl1yo] 3 times, yf, [brp1, sl1yof] 3 times, brp1, sl1yo, [brk1, yfsl1yo] twice, brk1, slip 1; turn.

Syncopated Row 10 LS DC: Hold LC across front of first st, then with DC, p1, sl1yo, [brk1, yfsl1yo] 3 times, yf, [brp1, sl1yof] twice, brp1, sl1yo, [brk1, yfsl1yo] twice, brk1, yf, sl1yof, p1. Do not turn; slide.

Syncopated Row 10 LS LC: With LC in front, slip 1, [brp1, sl1yof), twice, brp1, sl1yo, [brk1, yfsl1yo] 3 times, brk1, yf, [sl1yof, brp1] 3 times, slip 1; turn.

Repeat Syncopated Rows 9 and 10, DC and LC, once.

REVERSE MOTIF

Work Syncopated Rows 7 and 8, DC and LC, twice; Syncopated Rows 5 and 6, DC and LC, twice; Syncopated Rows 3 and 4, DC and LC, twice; then Syncopated Rows 1 and 2, DC and LC, twice. Work even in Two-Color Brioche, beginning with Row 2 DS DC, until you have 44 counted LS rows (88 working rows) from last Syncopated Row, ending with Row 1 LS DC.

SHAPE HEADBAND

Decrease Row 1 LS LC: With LC in front, slip 1, yb, brk1, yf, slip 1, t1lyo2, brssk, [yfsl1yo, brk1] 4 times, yf, slip 1, t1ryo, brk2tog, slip st from cn to left-hand needle, yfsl2yo, brk1, yf, slip 1–19 sts remain; turn.

Decrease Row 1 DS DC: Bring LC to front, bring DC from underneath LC and k1, yfsl1yo, brssk, [yfsl1yo, brk1] 5 times, yfsl1yo, brk2tog, yfsl1yo, k1–19 sts remain. Do not turn; slide. Work even until you have 8 counted LC rows (16 worked rows) from first decrease, ending with Row 1 LS DC.

Decrease Row 2 LS LC: With LC in front, slip 1, yb, brk1, yf, slip 1, t1lyo2, brssk, [yfsl1yo, brk1] twice, yf , slip 1, t1ryo, brk2tog, slip st from cn to left-hand needle, yfsl2yo, brk1, yf, slip 1–15 sts remain; turn.

Decrease Row 2 DS DC: Bring LC to front, bring DC from underneath LC and k1, yfsl1yo, brssk, [yfsl1yo, brk1] 3 times, yfsl1yo, brk2tog, yfsl1yo, k1–13 sts remain. Do not turn; slide. Work even until you have 16 counted LC rows (32 worked rows) from first decrease, ending with Row 1 LS DC.

Decrease Row 3 LS LC: With LC in front, slip 1, yb, brk1, yf, slip 1, t1lyo2, brssk, yf, slip 2, slip next st to cn, hold to back, transfer last slipped st from right-hand needle to left-hand needle, yo, brk2tog, slip st from cn to left-hand needle, yfsl2yo, brk1, yf, slip 1–11 sts remain; turn.

Decrease Row 3 DS DC: Bring LC to front, bring DC from underneath LC and k1, yfsl1yo, brssk, yfsl1yo, brk1, yfsl1yo, brk2tog, yfsl1yo, k1–9 sts remain. Do not turn; slide. Work even until you have 24 counted LC rows (48 worked rows) from first decrease, ending with Row 1 DS LC.

SECOND TIE

Set-Up Row LS DC: P1, *k1, brp1; repeat from * to last 2 sts, k1, p1. Change to Striped Rib, beginning with Row 2 LC. Work even until Tie measures 6" from beginning of Tie, ending with Row 1 or 3 DC. BO all sts in pattern.

Weave in ends.

laced wrap

LAURA ZUKAITE

Stripes are usually casual and sporty, but Laura's delicate stitch pattern, soft colors, and elegant yarn choice make this striped feminine wrap appropriate for even a fancy evening out. Her use of laces in the design further blurs the distinction between casual and dressy.

FINISHED MEASUREMENTS

25" circumference at narrowest point x 10½" long

YARN

Artyarns Silk Mohair (70% super kid mohair / 30% silk; 230 yards / 25 grams): 1 hank #250 (A)
Artyarns Silk Rhapsody (100% silk core wrapped with 70% mohair / 30% silk; 260 yards / 100 grams): 2 hanks #149 (B)

NEEDLES

1 pair straight needles size US 9 (5.5 mm)
Change needle size if necessary to obtain correct gauge.

NOTIONS

4 yds ⅜" wide ribbon

GAUGE

16 sts and 75 rows = 4" (10 cm) in Fold Pattern, changing yarns as indicated

STITCH PATTERN

FOLD PATTERN

(any number of sts; 14-row repeat) *Note: Do not break yarn when changing yarns. Carry yarn not in use up outside edge.*
Set-Up Rows 1, 3, and 5: With A, purl.
Set-Up Rows 2 and 4: Knit.
Set-Up Row 6: *Slip 1 st purlwise, with right-hand needle, pick up 1 corresponding CO st from back of st, k2tog (slipped st together with picked-up st); repeat from * to end.
Rows 1, 3, and 5: Change to B. Knit.
Rows 2, 4, and 6: Purl.

Row 7 (Fold Row): Change to A. *Slip 1 st purlwise, with right-hand needle, pick up 1 corresponding color B st from 6 rows below, k2tog (slipped st together with picked-up st); repeat from * to end.
Rows 8, 10, and 12: Continuing in A, knit.
Rows 9, 11, and 13: Purl.
Row 14 (Fold Row): *Slip 1 st purlwise, with right-hand needle, pick up 1 corresponding color A st from 6 rows below, k2tog (slipped st together with picked-up st); repeat from * to end.
Repeat Rows 1-14 for Fold Pattern; do not repeat Set-Up Rows 1-6. *Note: The instructions will have you work until a specified number of folds have been completed. Set-Up Row 6, and Rows 7 and 14 each complete a fold; Rows 1 and 8 begin the next fold. Set-Up Row 6 and Row 14 complete color A folds on the first side. Row 7 completes a color B fold on the opposite side. Be sure to count folds on both sides when working the instructions.*

WRAP

Using A, CO 150 sts; begin Fold Pattern. Work even until 4 folds have been completed.
***Decrease Row:** Decrease 5 sts evenly spaced across first row of next fold–145 sts remain. Work even for 6 rows; fold should be complete. Repeat last 7 rows once–140 sts remain. Work even for 14 rows; 2 folds should be completed without shaping.

Repeat from * 4 times; you should have worked a total of 10 decrease rows and 24 folds from the beginning. Work even until 4 more folds are complete, binding off all sts on Row 7 of last fold.

FINISHING

Lace ribbon through side edges of folds, working from narrow to wide end. Tie at wide end.

incognita

Bonnie's clever design is two fashionable hats in one and the epitome of reversibility. When worn with the brim to the front and the scarf twisted into a cowl, Incognita lends an aura of mystery (see right). When it is turned inside out with the brim to the back and the scarf twisted around the crown, it transforms into an exotic turban (see page 145).

SIZE
Adult women's Small/Medium (Medium/Large)
Shown in size Small/Medium

FINISHED MEASUREMENTS
17¾ (19½)" circumference

YARN
Malabrigo Chunky (100% merino wool; 104 yards / 100 gram hank): 3 hanks Bobby Blue

NEEDLES
One set of five double-pointed needles (dpn) size US 11 (8 mm)
One 16" (40 cm) long circular (circ) needle size US 11 (8 mm)
One 24" (60 cm) long circular needle size US 11 (8 mm)
Change needle size if necessary to obtain correct gauge.

NOTIONS
Crochet hook size US L-11 (8 mm); waste yarn in superbulky weight; stitch marker; removable markers; tapestry needle

GAUGE
10¼ sts and 20½ rows = 4" (10 cm) in Garter st (knit every row), using 2 strands of yarn held together

STITCH PATTERNS

K2, P2 RIB
(multiple of 4 sts; 1-rnd repeat)
All Rnds: *K2, p2; repeat from * to end.

SCARF PATTERN
(any number of sts; 4-rnd repeat)
Rnds 1 and 2: Purl.
Rnds 3 and 4: Knit.
Repeat Rnds 1-4 for Scarf Pattern.

NOTES
The Hat is totally reversible. However, for the purposes of the instructions, one side will be labeled RS and the other side WS.

HAT

BRIM
Using waste yarn, dpns and Provisional CO (see page 178), CO 8 sts. Bring yarn to back and slip loop from crochet hook onto needle–9 sts. Change to 2 strands of working yarn held together and Garter st (knit every row), leaving an 18" tail. Work even for 89 (97) rows [44 (48) ridges], ending with a RS row.
Note: You may want to place a removable marker at the beginning of the first row to mark the RS. Piece should measure approximately 17½ (19)" from the beginning. Do not break yarn.

With WS facing, beginning at end with 18" tail, carefully unravel Provisional CO and place 9 sts on separate dpn. Pass next-to-last st over last st and off needle–8 sts remain. Slip sts to right-hand end of needle. With tapestry needle threaded with 2 strands of tail, bring tail over dpn to back, then insert tapestry needle through st that yarn is coming from, making a new st–9 sts. This is now the back needle for grafting. Bring up remaining needle so that needles are parallel, with Provisional CO needle in the back, and the tail yarn coming from the right-hand end. Working with tail yarn, graft sts together as follows, keeping grafted sts even as you work:

Step 1. Thread tapestry needle through first st on front needle knitwise, leaving st on needle.

Step 2. Working on sts on back needle, thread tapestry needle through first st purlwise, slipping st off needle, then through second st knitwise, leaving st on needle.

Step 3. Repeat Step 2, working on sts on front needle.

Repeat Steps 2 and 3 until 1 st remains on each needle. Thread tapestry needle through last st on back needle knitwise, slipping st off needle, then through last st on front needle purlwise, slipping st off needle.

CROWN

Note: Change to dpn when necessary for number of sts on needle. Place removeable marker at end of grafted row, between two purl ridges, for center back of Brim. With RS facing, using 16" circ needle and 2 strands of working yarn from Brim (not tail yarn) held together, beginning at marker, pick up and knit 1 st in each purl ridge along right side edge of Brim–45 (49) sts. Join for working in the rnd; pm for beginning of rnd. Purl 1 rnd, decreasing 1 st at beginning of rnd–44 (48) sts remain. Knit 1 rnd. Change to K2, P2 Rib. Work even for 2 (2¼)", or to 1½" shorter than desired Crown depth.

Shape Crown

Rnd 1: *K2tog, p2tog; repeat from * to end–22 (24) sts remain.

Rnds 2 and 4: Knit the knit sts and purl the purl sts as they face you.

Rnd 3: *K2tog, p2tog; repeat from * to last 2 (4) sts, k2tog (k2tog, p2tog)–11 (12) sts remain.

Rnd 5: *K2tog; repeat from * to last 1 (2) st(s), k1 (k2tog)–6 sts remain. Break yarn, leaving a long tail. Thread tail through remaining sts, pull tight and fasten off, with tail to WS.

EAR COZY SCARF

Place marker 15 (16) purl ridges from each side of center back of Brim, along remaining side of Brim. With RS facing, using 24" circ needle and 1 strand of yarn, pick up and knit 30 (32) sts between markers.

Shape Ear Cozy Scarf

Note: Ear Cozy Scarf is shaped using short rows (see Short-Row Shaping, page 186).

Row 1 (WS): K11, w&t.

Rows 2, 4, and 6: Knit to end.

Row 3: K7, w&t.

Row 5: K3, w&t.

Row 7: Knit across all sts, working wraps together with wrapped sts as you come to them.

Rows 8-14: Repeat Rows 1-7, working short rows on RS rows, and ending with a RS row.

Row 15: AO-f 1 st, CO 71 sts using Cable CO (see page 178)–102 (104) sts. *Note: When working the Cable CO, be sure to place newly CO sts onto the needle purlwise.* Turn work so RS is now facing. Join for working in the rnd, p1, pass last CO st over purled st; pm for beginning of rnd–101 (103) sts remain.

Next Rnd: Knit to 1 st before CO sts, removing all markers, k2, pso, knit to end–100 (102) sts remain. Change to Scarf Pattern. Work Rnds 1-4 three times, then Rnds 1-3 once. BO all sts knitwise.

VISOR

When you hold the Hat with RS of front of Brim facing you, each purl ridge of the Brim will now form a vertical column. Each column is divided into two sides, which are comprised of half-moons, one half-moon facing right and one facing left. When picking up sts for the Visor, you will be picking up in the right and/or left half-moons. Place markers 2 columns to each side of open edge of Brim [the edge between the picked-up ends of the Ear Cozy Scarf – you should have a total of 20 (22) columns between markers]. Place markers on 6th column in from each marker, in 10th half-moon up from edge of Brim.

With RS of Brim facing, holding Hat upside down so that Crown is closest to you, using 24" long circ needle and 2 strands of yarn held together, pick up and knit 29 (31) sts as follows: 9 sts on the diagonal in columns 1-5, picking up in left half-moon of first st in first column, [in right half-moon, then left half-moon in next st toward top of Hat in next column to the left] 4 times (see illustration below–green sts); 11 (13) sts straight across in right-half moons in columns 6-16 (18) (blue sts); and 9 sts on the diagonal in columns 16-20 (18-22), picking up in left half-moon of column 16 (18), [in right half-moon, then left half-moon in next st toward edge of Brim in next column to the right] 4 times (red sts). Remove markers.

Shape Visor
Note: Visor is shaped using short rows.
Rows 1 and 2: Knit to last 2 sts, w&t.
Rows 3 and 4: Knit to last 3 sts, w&t.
Rows 5 and 6: Knit to last 5 sts, w&t.
Rows 7 and 8: Knit to last 6 sts, w&t.
Rows 9 and 10: Knit to last 8 sts, w&t.
Rows 11 and 12: Knit to end, working wraps together with wrapped sts as you come to them.

FINISHING

Tack down the first picked-up st and last bound-off st of the Visor. Weave in ends, weaving single strands in different directions to make them less noticeable.

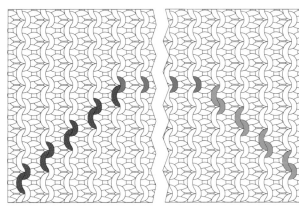

Working the Visor

NORAH GAUGHAN

reverse me

Aptly named, Norah's cardigan begs to be worn any which way you choose–right-side up or upside down and inside or out–as either a long hip-hugging jacket (see right) or a short jacket with a generous shawl collar (see page 149). Crocheted seams combined with Norah's wonderful and generously textured reversible stitch pattern play a significant role in why the cardigan can be worn so many different ways.

SIZE

X-Small (Small, Medium, Large)
To fit busts size 28-32 (34-38, 40-44, 46-50)"
Shown in size Medium

FINISHED MEASUREMENTS

37 (42½, 48, 54½)" chest

YARN

Berroco Ultra Alpaca (50% superfine alpaca / 50% Peruvian highland wool; 100 grams / 215 yards): 9 (10, 11, 12) hanks #6249 Fennel

NEEDLES

One pair straight needles size US 7 (4.5 mm)
Change needle size if necessary to obtain correct gauge.

NOTIONS

Crochet hook size E-4 (3.5 mm); eight 1" buttons

GAUGE

20 sts and 26 rows = 4" (10 cm) in Stockinette stitch (St st)

NOTES

The Cardigan is worked in 7 pieces: Back/Sleeves, Right Front/Sleeve, Left Front/Sleeve, Sleeve Cuffs (2), Collar, and Bottom Band. The Cardigan is completely reversible. However, for the purposes of the instructions, each piece will have a RS and a WS.

BACK/SLEEVES

CO 92 (106, 120, 136) sts; begin St st, beginning with a purl row. Work even until piece measures 8 (8, 8½, 8½)" from the beginning, ending with a WS (purl) row.
Shape Sleeves (RS): Increase 1 st each side this row, then every other row twice, ending with a WS row. CO 2 sts at beginning of next 6 rows, 4 sts at beginning of next 6 rows, then 12 (12, 14, 14) sts at beginning of next 2 rows–158 (172, 190, 206) sts. Work even until piece measures 17 (17, 17½, 17½)" from the beginning, ending with a WS row.
Shape Shoulders (RS): BO 9 (9, 11, 12) sts at beginning of next 8 rows, then 7 (10, 11, 13) sts at beginning of next 4 rows. BO remaining 58 (60, 58, 58) sts for Back neck.

RIGHT FRONT/SLEEVE

CO 3 sts; begin St st, beginning with a purl row. Work even for 1 row.
Shape Bottom Edge (RS): Continuing in St st, CO 2 (2, 2, 3) sts at beginning of this row, then every other row 5 (9, 12, 11) times–15 (23, 29, 39) sts. Work even until piece measures same as for Back to beginning of Sleeve shaping, ending with a WS row.
Shape Sleeves (RS): Increase 1 st at end of this row, then every other row twice–18 (26, 32, 42) sts. Work even for 2 rows.
Next Row (WS): CO 2 sts at beginning of this row, 2 sts at beginning of next 2 WS rows, 4 sts at beginning of next 3 WS rows, then 12 (12, 14, 14) sts at beginning of next WS row–48 (56, 64, 74) sts. Work even until piece measures same as for Back to shoulder shaping, shape shoulder as for Back.

LEFT FRONT/SLEEVE

Work as for Right Front/Sleeve, reversing all shaping, and working only 1 row even before beginning Sleeve cast-ons.

CUFFS

CO 67 sts; begin Cable Pattern from Chart. Work even until piece measures 12" from the beginning. BO all sts in pattern. *Note: You may want to work some sts together when binding off to keep edge from flaring.*

COLLAR

Work as for Cuffs until piece measures 45½ (43½, 42, 42½)" from the beginning. BO all sts in pattern.

BOTTOM BAND

Work as for Cuffs until piece measures 36 (42, 47, 53)" from the beginning. BO all sts in pattern.

FINISHING

Using Seam Join as described below, work seams in the following order: join shoulders; join Cuffs to Sleeves; join sides and underside of Sleeves and Cuffs; join Collar to Right Front, Back neck, and Left Front; join Bottom Band to lower edge of body. *Note: When joining the Bottom Band to the body, ease Bottom Band slightly across Back.*

Seam Join: With RSs of pieces to be joined held together, using crochet hook, work single crochet along raw edges of both pieces, alternating 1 single crochet into piece facing you with 1 single crochet into piece facing away from you. *Note: Always work into WS of piece; do not go between pieces to work into RS of piece facing away from you.*

Crochet Edging: Place markers for 4 button loops along center edge of Right Front Bottom Band, beginning and ending 1" in from either edge of Bottom Band. With RS facing, using crochet hook, work single crochet along entire edge of garment, working button loops at markers, as follows:

Button Loops: Chain 7, join with slip st to edge.
Sew buttons opposite button loops, on both RS and WS, 1" in from edge.

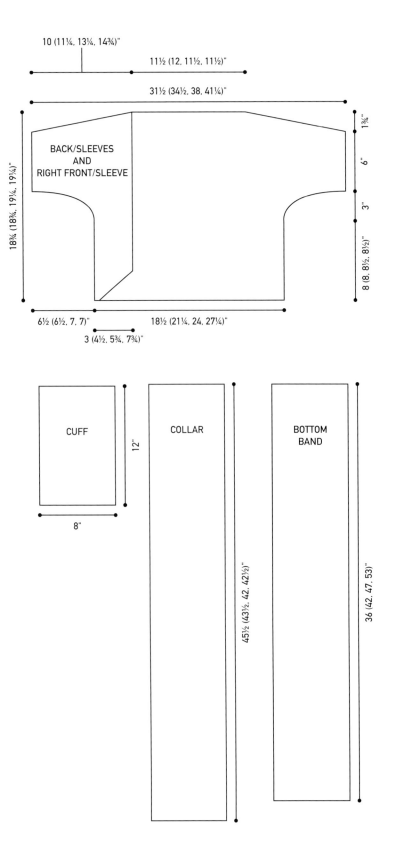

CABLE PATTERN

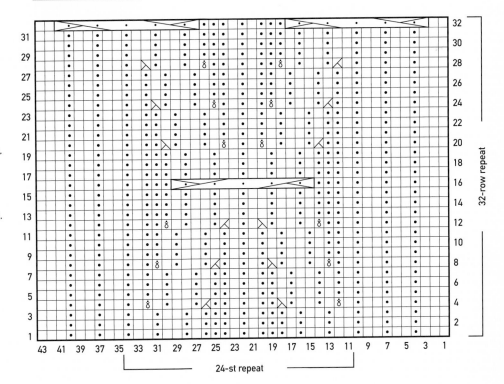

24-st repeat

32-row repeat

VÉRONIK AVERY

lice jacket

Véronik has a gift for designing pieces that are both timeless and contemporary, and this jacket is a perfect example. She has revamped traditional folk motifs into a thoroughly modern, elegantly tailored jacket with minimalist lines. It's worked in an inverse-color double knit, producing a strikingly different look on each side. The sharp contrast between the light and dark colors offers both extroverted and introverted options to suit either mood.

SIZES
X-Small (Small, Medium, Large, X-Large)
Shown in size Small

FINISHED MEASUREMENTS
32½ (36, 39½, 44, 47½)" chest, overlapped

YARN
Reynolds Lite Lopi (100% wool; 109 yards / 50 grams):
8 (9, 10, 11, 11) balls each #0054 Ash Heather (A) and
#0429 Berry Heather (B)

NEEDLES
One 32" (80 cm) long or longer circular (circ) needle size
US 3 (3.25 mm)
One set of five double-pointed needles (dpn) size
US 3 (3.25 mm)
Change needle size if necessary to obtain correct gauge.

NOTIONS
Cable needle (cn); stitch holders; stitch markers
(one in contrasting color)

GAUGE
18 sts and 25 rows = 4" (10 cm) in Stockinette stitch (St st)
worked using the double knitting method (see page 181)

NOTES
This Jacket is worked in double knitting throughout, and all stitches are worked in pairs. When instructions call for a number of stitches to be worked, work that number of stitch pairs. For example, if instructed to work 10 sts, you will [knit one stitch, purl 1 stitch] 10 times.

To ensure neat edges when working in rows, cross the strands at the beginning of every row.

The Jacket is totally reversible. However, for the purposes of the instructions, the side using A as the main color will be labeled RS, and the other side WS.

ABBREVIATIONS
Dbl inc (double st increase): Work 2 yo's, each one using 1 of the 2 strands. Knit each yo through the back loop (tbl) on the return row or rnd.

Dbl ssk (double st ssk decrease): Slip next knit st to right-hand needle; slip next purl st to cn, hold to back. Return knit st to left-hand needle and, using same color yarn as facing side and holding both strands in back, ssk. Return purl st to left-hand needle and, using opposite color yarn as facing side and holding both strands in front, p2tog.

Dbl k2tog (double st k2tog decrease): Slip next knit st to right-hand needle; slip next purl st to cn, hold to back. Return knit st to left-hand needle and, using same color yarn as facing side and holding both strands in back, k2tog. Return purl st to left-hand needle and, using opposite color yarn as facing side and holding both strands in front, ssp.

Hide Gaps: Work to last st before gap (2 yo's on left-hand needle) and hide gap as follows: Slip next yo to right-hand needle; slip next yo to cn, hold to back. Return first yo to left-hand needle and k2tog; return yo on cn to left-hand needle and p2tog.

BODY

Using circ needle, A and B, and Tubular Two-Color CO (see page 180), CO 173 (189, 205, 229, 245) sts in each color–346 (378, 410, 458, 490) sts. Begin double-knit St st (see page 181); work even for 4 rows.

Begin Lice Pattern (RS): K2, work Lice Pattern from Chart across 169 (185, 201, 225, 241) sts, ending as indicated in Chart, k2. Work even until piece measures approximately 10½ (10¾, 11¼, 11½, 11¾)" from the beginning, ending with Row 6 of Lice Pattern.

Begin Back Medallion (RS): Work 68 (76, 84, 96, 104) sts as established, place marker (pm), work Row 1 of Back Medallion from Chart across 37 sts, pm, work Lice Pattern as established to end. Work even until piece measures 10¾ (11, 11½, 11¾, 12)" from the beginning ending with a ws row.

Divide for Fronts and Back (RS): Work 48 (51, 54, 58, 61) sts, pm, work 4 (6, 8, 14, 16) sts, place these sts on holder for right underarm, pm, work across 69 (75, 81, 85, 91) Back sts, pm, work 4 (6, 8, 14, 16) sts, place these sts on holder for left underarm, pm, work to end. Do not break yarn. Set aside. Note on which row of Lice Pattern you ended; you will need to end on this same row for the Sleeves.

SLEEVES

Using circ needle, A and B, and Tubular Two-Color CO, CO 45 sts in each color–90 sts. Join for working in the rnd, being careful not to twist sts; pm for beginning of rnd. Begin double-knit St st; work even for 4 rows.

Begin Lice Pattern: K2, work Lice Pattern from Chart across 41 sts, k2. Work even for 5 rnds.

Begin Cuff Pattern: K2, work Cuff Pattern from Chart across 41 sts, ending as indicated in Chart, k2. Work even for 7 rnds. Change to Lice Pattern, beginning with Rnd 2 of Chart. Work even until piece measures 6" from the beginning.

Shape Sleeve: Increase 2 sts this rnd, every 12 (8, 6, 4, 4) rnds 2 (1, 1, 3, 8) time(s), then every 14 (10, 8, 6, 6) rnds 3 (6, 8, 10, 7) times, as follows: K1, dbl inc, work to last st, dbl inc, k1–57 (61, 65, 73, 77) sts. Work even until piece measures 17½ (18, 18½, 18¾, 19¼)" from the beginning, ending on same rnd of Lice Pattern as for Body. Place first and last 2 (3, 4, 7, 8) sts on holder for underarm–53 (55, 57, 59, 61) sts remain. Break yarn and set aside.

YOKE

With WS facing, using yarn attached to Body, work across 48 (51, 54, 58, 61) sts for Left Front, slip marker (sm), 53 (55, 57, 59, 61) sts for Left Sleeve, sm, 69 (75, 81, 85, 91) sts for Back, sm, 53 (55, 57, 59, 61) sts for Right Sleeve, sm, and 48 (51, 54, 58, 61) sts for Right Front–271 (287, 303, 319, 335) sts.

SHAPE RAGLAN YOKE

Size X-Small Only

Row 1 (RS): [Work to 2 sts before next marker, dbl ssk, sm, dbl k2tog] 4 times, work to end–263 sts remain.

Row 2: Work even.

Row 3: [Work to next marker, sm, dbl k2tog, work to 2 sts before next marker, dbl ssk, sm] twice, work to end–259 sts remain.

Row 4: Work even.

Rows 5-8: Repeat Rows 1-4–247 sts remain.

Rows 9-10: Repeat Rows 3 and 4–243 sts remain.

Repeat Rows 1-10 twice, Rows 1-4 once, then Rows 3 and 4 once–171 sts remain (41 sts each Front, 17 sts each Sleeve, 55 sts for Back).

Sizes (Small, Medium, Large, X-Large)

Row 1 (RS): [Work to 2 sts before next marker, dbl ssk, sm, dbl k2tog] 4 times, work to end–(279, 295, 311, 327) sts remain.

Row 2: Work even.

Row 3: [Work to next marker, sm, dbl k2tog, work to 2 sts before next marker, dbl ssk, sm] twice, work to end–(275, 291, 307, 323) sts remain.

Row 4: Work even.

Repeat Rows 1-4 eight times, work to end–(179, 195, 211, 227) sts remain [(42, 45, 49, 52) sts each Front, (19, 21, 23, 25) sts each Sleeve, (57, 63, 67, 73) sts for Back].

All sts worked in double-knit St st.

 A

B

CUFF PATTERN

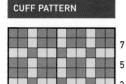

7
5
3
1

8-rnd repeat

11 9 7 5 3 1

6-st
repeat

LICE PATTERN

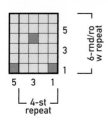

5
3
1

6-rnd/ro
w repeat

5 3 1

4-st
repeat

BACK MEDALLION

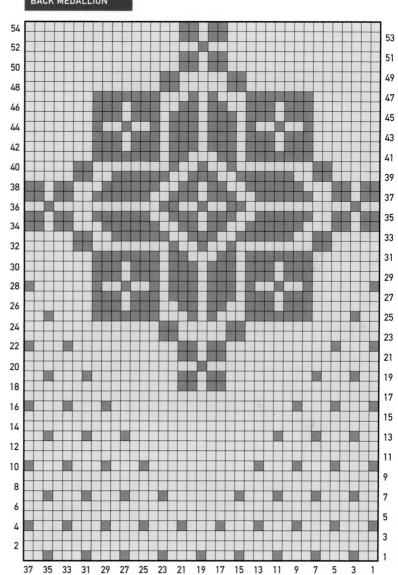

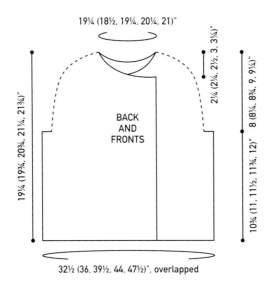

19¼ (18½, 19¼, 20¼, 21)"

2¼ (2¼, 2½, 2½, 3, 3¼)"

8 (8¼, 8¾, 9, 9¼)"

BACK
AND
FRONTS

19¼ (19¾, 20¾, 21¼, 21¾)"

10¾ (11, 11½, 11¾, 12)"

32½ (36, 39½, 44, 47½)", overlapped

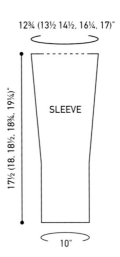

12¾ (13½ 14½, 16¼, 17)"

SLEEVE

17½ (18, 18½, 18¾, 19¼)"

10"

All Sizes

SHAPE SHOULDERS AND SLEEVES

Row 1 (RS): [Work to 2 sts before next marker, dbl ssk, sm, dbl k2tog] 4 times, work to end–163 (171, 187, 203, 219) sts remain.

Row 2: [Work to 2 sts before next marker, dbl ssk, sm, work to next marker, sm, dbl k2tog] twice, work to end–159 (167, 183, 199, 215) sts remain.

Repeat Rows 1 and 2 six (seven, eight, nine, ten) times and AT THE SAME TIME, when piece measures 17 (17½, 18¼, 18¼, 18½)" from the beginning, ending with a WS row, begin neck shaping.

SHAPE NECK

Rows 1 (RS) and 2: Continuing with shoulder and Sleeve shaping, work to last 12 sts, turn; dbl inc, work to last 12 sts, turn.

Rows 3 and 4: [Dbl inc, work to last 4 sts before gap (including yo from previous row), turn] twice.

Repeat Rows 3 and 4 four (three, two, two, one) time(s).

Sizes (Small, Medium, Large, X-Large) Only

Rows 5 (WS) and 6: [Dbl inc, work to last 3 sts before gap (including dbl yo from previous row), turn] twice.

Repeat Rows 5 and 6 (zero, two, three, five) times.

All Sizes

Next Row (RS): Working across all sts and hiding all gaps on first 2 rows, continue shaping shoulders and Sleeves until all decreases have been completed, ending with a WS row–87 (83, 87, 91, 95) sts remain [27 (26, 27, 29, 30) sts each Front, 3 sts each Sleeve, 27 (25, 27, 27, 29) sts for Back]. Break A, leaving a length 4 times as long as neckline.

Next Row: Using B, purl 1 row, slipping all knit sts wyib. Break B. Do not turn work. Using A and K1, P1 Bind-Off with Kitchener (see page 184), BO all sts.

FINISHING

Using Kitchener st (see page 183), graft underarm sts of Sleeves and Body. Weave in all ends. Block piece to measurements.

PAM ALLEN

brioche bag

Jazz up your everyday look with Pam's bold, bohemian-style bag. Worked in an easy Stockinette and two-color brioche, this casual yet striking bag appears to reverse into two seemingly different palettes, though both sides use the same four colors (see below and page 156). Worked in the round without increases or decreases while working the brioche, this design is a great introduction for anyone new to the technique.

FINISHED MEASUREMENTS

Approximately 11" in diameter by 14" high, not including Straps

YARN

Classic Elite Yarns Montera Heathers (50% llama / 50% wool; 127 yards / 100 grams): 1 hank each #3844 Bronze Medal (A), #3874 Sycamore (B), #3830 Paisley Plum (C), and #3847 Copper (D)

NEEDLES

One 24" (60 cm) long circular (circ) needle size US 9 (5.5 mm)
One 16" (40 cm) long circular needle size US 9 (5.5 mm)
One 24" (60 cm) long circular needle size US 7 (4.5 mm)
One set of five double-pointed needles (dpn) size US 9 (5.5 mm)
One set of five double-pointed needles (dpn) size US 6 (4 mm)
Change needle size if necessary to obtain correct gauge.

NOTIONS

Stitch markers; waste yarn; tapestry needle

GAUGE

15 sts and 24 rows = 4" (10 cm) in Stockinette stitch (St st), using size US 7 (4.5 mm) needles

NOTES

This Bag is totally reversible. However, for the purposes of the instructions, one side will be labeled RS and the other side WS.

The Body of the Bag is cast on with waste yarn and worked in-the-round in Two-Color Brioche Rib. Each round is worked with only one color; A rounds are knit with A, and B rounds are purled with B. A rounds alternate with B rounds. The Top of the Bag is worked in double knitting to the beginning of the Straps, the front and back of which are worked separately to the end, then sewn together along the side edges. The Base of the Bag is worked down from the waste yarn cast-on edge. The edges of the Straps are finished with an I-Cord trim.

STITCH PATTERNS

When working yo's in Two-Color Brioche Rib, work them as follows:

Slip 1, yo, followed by k2tog: Using A, bring yarn to front, slip 1 st (B); leaving yarn in front, k2tog the next st (A) and following yo (B). A yo automatically forms when you bring the yarn over the needle to work the k2tog.

Slip 1, yo, followed by p2tog: Using B, with yarn in front, slip 1 st (A), bring yarn over needle and under again to front, ready to p2tog the next st (B) and following yo (A).

TWO-COLOR BRIOCHE RIB

(multiple of 2 sts; 2-rnd repeat)

Set-Up Rnd: *K1, slip 1 (B) wyif, yo; repeat from * to end. *Note: Wrap last yo strand over needle, then between needles to front. Leave it in front until end of next rnd.*

Rnd 1: Change to B. *Slip 1 (A) wyif, yo, p2tog [slipped st (B) from previous rnd together with its yo (A)]; repeat from * to end, working last st together with loose strand of A, leaving yarn in front after last st.

Rnd 2: Change to A. *K2tog [slipped st (A) from previous rnd together with its yo (B)], slip 1 (B) wyif, yo; repeat from * to end, working last yo as for Set-Up Rnd.

Repeat Rnds 1 and 2 for Two-Color Brioche Rib.

DOUBLE KNITTING PATTERN

(multiple of 2 sts; 2-rnd repeat)

Set-Up Row 1: *K2tog [slipped st (C) from previous rnd together with its yo (D)], pick up and knit into purl bump C below next purl st on needle, slip 1 (D) wyif; repeat from * to end, leaving yarn in front after last st. Turn work so WS is facing you, with sts just finished farthest from you. *Note: You should now have twice as many C sts as D sts.*

Set-Up Row 2: Change to D. *K1, slip 1 (C) wyif, pick up and knit into purl bump D below next purl st on needle, slip 1 (C) wyif; repeat from * to end, leaving yarn to WS after last st. Turn work so RS is facing you, with sts just finished nearest you. Yarn C should be in front; D should be to WS. *Note: You should now have twice as many sts as before beginning Set-Up Row 1.*

Rnd 1: Change to C. *K1, slip 1 (D) wyif; repeat from * to end, leaving yarn in front after last st.

Rnd 2: Change to D. *Slip 1 (C) wyib, p1; repeat from * to end, leaving yarn in back after last st.

Repeat Rnds 1 and 2 for Double Knitting Pattern.

BAG

BODY

Using longer size US 9 circ needle, waste yarn and Provisional CO (see page 178), CO 80 sts. Change to B. Knit 1 row. Join for working in the rnd, being careful not to twist sts; place marker (pm) for beginning of rnd. Change to A; begin Two-Color Brioche Rib. Work even until piece measures 12" from the beginning, ending with Rnd 2 of Two-Color Brioche. Change to Colors C and D, using C in place of A and D in place of B. Work even for 1", ending with Rnd 1 of Two-Color Brioche Rib.

TOP

Change to size US 7 circ needle, C, and Double Knitting Pattern. Work even until piece measures 1½" from beginning of Double Knitting Pattern, ending with Rnd 2.

Shape Top: Change to C. Work 36 sts as established (18 C sts and 18 D sts), BO next 8 sts as follows: [Ssk (1 C st together with 1 D st)] twice, pso, [ssk, pso] twice, pso 1 C st. Work 35 sts, beginning with slip 1 (D) st, BO next 8 sts as above, work to end—144 sts remain (36 C sts and 36 D sts each side). Break yarn.

Begin Strap

Set-Up: Thread a tapestry needle with waste yarn. With RS facing, beginning at BO sts, separate C side from D side by slipping C sts to needle and D sts to waste yarn—36 C sts on needle, 36 D sts on waste yarn. Transfer remaining 36 C sts and 36 D sts separately to waste yarn. Set aside.

Shape Strap (RS): Working back and forth on C sts only, join C and BO 2 sts at beg of next 4 rows, decrease 1 st each side every other row 6 times, then every 4 rows 3 times—10 sts remain. Work even until Strap measures 12", or to desired length from beginning of shaping. Transfer sts to waste yarn and set aside. Turn work so that St st side of D sts is facing. Transfer 36 D sts from waste yarn to needle. Join D and shape as for C side. Repeat for opposite side Straps.

BASE

Note: Change to dpns when necessary for number of sts on needle. Carefully unravel waste yarn from CO edge and transfer 80 sts to shorter size US 9 circ needle. Join for working in the rnd; pm for beginning of rnd.

Rnd 1: *K2tog; repeat from * to end of rnd—40 sts remain.

Rnds 2 and 4: Purl.

Rnds 3 and 5: Repeat Rnd 1—10 sts remain after Rnd 5. Break yarn, thread tail through remaining sts twice, pull tight and fasten off.

FINISHING

With RSs together, sew C and D sides of Straps together, working st for st on the straight edges, and working along the curves as best you can. Press Straps and Top of Bag with steam iron. Using Kitchener st (see Kitchener Plus, page 183), graft top of Straps together.

I-Cord Trim (make 2): Using smaller dpn and C, CO 3 sts. *Transfer needle with sts to left hand, bring yarn around behind work to right-hand side; using second dpn, knit sts from right to left, pulling yarn from left to right for first st; do not turn. Slide sts to opposite end of needle; repeat from * until piece is long enough to fit around entire Strap opening. Fasten off. Sew I-Cord along BO sts of Top and Strap seams.

flip your lid

With just a flick of the wrist to add a twist to the middle of the knitted hourglass shape, Eric's versatile hat can change from a textured plum solid into a contrasting white lace (or vice versa). Offset the twist and turn the longer side up, and you have two more options with contrasting colored brims – four hats in one.

FINISHED MEASUREMENTS

21" circumference

YARN

Green Mountain Spinnery Sock Art Meadow (50% fine kid mohair / 50% fine wool; 400 yards / 4 ounces): 1 hank Undyed Natural White (A)

Green Mountain Spinnery Sock Art Forest (70% fine wool/ 30% Tencel®; 400 yards / 4 ounces): 1 hank Plum (B)

NEEDLES

One 16" (40 cm) long circular (circ) needle size US 4 (3.5 mm)

One set of five double-pointed needles (dpn) size US 4 (3.5 mm)

Change needle size if necessary to obtain correct gauge.

NOTIONS

Stitch markers; cable needle (cn)

GAUGE

24 sts and 38 rnds = 4" (10 cm) in Stockinette stitch (St st)

HAT

Note: Change to dpns when necessary for number of sts on needle.
Using circ needle and A, CO 123 sts. Join for working in the rnd, being careful not to twist sts; place marker (pm) for beginning of rnd. Begin Garter st (purl 1 rnd, knit 1 rnd); work even for 6 rnds.

Begin Charts: [Work 30 sts from Chart A, pm, work 11 sts from Chart B, pm] 3 times. Working Charts between markers as established, work Chart rnds as follows:

Chart A: Rnds 1-18 three times, Rnds 19-36 once, working decreases as indicated, Rnds 37-46 twice, then Rnds 37-41 once;

Chart B: Rnds 1-8 once, then repeat Rnds 3-8 until Chart A rnds are complete, ending with Rnd 7 of Chart B, and removing markers on last rnd—87 sts remain.

Next Rnd: Change to B. [Work 18 sts from Chart C, pm, work 11 sts from Chart D, pm] 3 times. Working Charts between markers as established, work Chart rnds as follows:

Chart C: Rnds 1-10 twice, Rnds 11-24 once, working increases as indicated, then Rnds 25-42 three times; **Chart D:** Rnds 1-10 once, then repeat Rnds 3-10 until Chart C rnds are complete, ending with Rnd 8 of Chart D, and removing markers on last rnd—123 sts.

Next Rnd: Change to Garter st; work even for 6 rnds. BO all sts knitwise.

KEY	
□	Knit
•	Purl
O	Yo
⊠	K1-tbl
⊠	K2tog
⊠	Slip 1 st knitwise, slip 1 st purlwise, k2tog-tbl.
⊠	M1
■	No stitch
⊠	Slip 1 st to cn, hold to back, k1, k1 from cn.
⊠	Slip 1 st to cn, hold to front, k1, k1 from cn.

CHART C

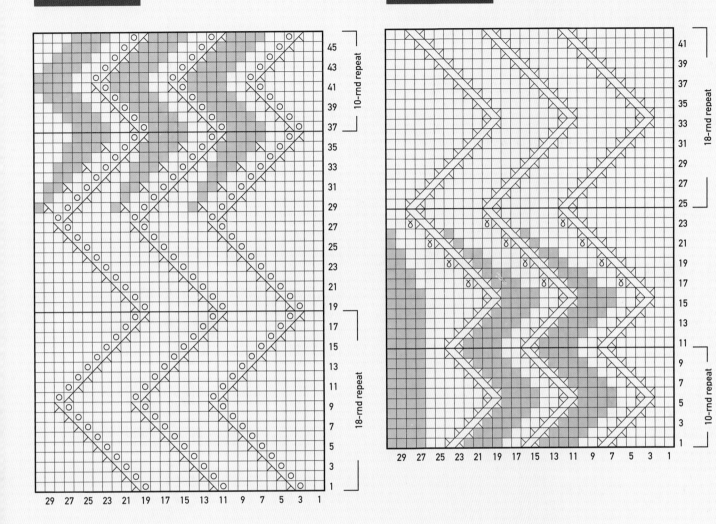

10-rnd repeat

18-rnd repeat

18-rnd repeat

10-rnd repeat

45 43 41 39 37 35 33 31 29 27 25 23 21 19 17 15 13 11 9 7 5 3 1

29 27 25 23 21 19 17 15 13 11 9 7 5 3 1

41 39 37 35 33 31 29 27 25 23 21 19 17 15 13 11 9 7 5 3 1

29 27 25 23 21 19 17 15 13 11 9 7 5 3 1

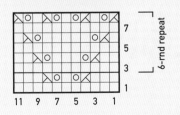

6-rnd repeat

7 5 3 1

11 9 7 5 3 1

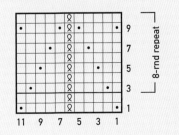

8-rnd repeat

9 7 5 3 1

11 9 7 5 3 1

tie socks

LYNNE BARR

Although bikinis were not my inspiration, that's what I thought of when I first tied on a pair of these socks. They show some skin in the middle, and the ties feel similar to the tie sides of a string bikini. The socks were inspired by the Looping Rib stitch (see page 32), and are knit with one continuous strand from the top of the ties to the tip of the toes. They can be worn three ways—as an identical matched pair, or turn just one of these reversible socks inside out to pair with the other for two different mirrored looks.

SIZES

One size

Note: These Socks are extremely stretchy because of the ribbing and the elastic content of the yarn used, and should fit a very wide range of sizes. Try the Socks on as you go. If you are using a yarn without elastic and would like to add length to the Foot or Ties, the instructions indicate where to do so.

YARN

Knit One Crochet Two Soxx Appeal (96% superwash merino wool / 3% nylon / 1% elastic; 208 yards / 50 grams): 2 balls #9419 Toffee (Single Tie version) or #9577 Avocado (Two-Tie version)

NEEDLES

One 16" (40 cm) long or longer circular (circ) needle size US 3 (3.25 mm)
One set of five double-pointed needles (dpn) size US 3 (3.25 mm)
Change needle size if necessary to obtain correct gauge.

GAUGE

30 sts and 29 rows = 3" (7.5 cm) in K1, P1 Rib

NOTES

These Socks are worked flat in one piece beginning at the back of the ankle (see A in photo), and worked through two sets of ties for the two-tie version (see B and C) or just the first set of ties (omit C) for the Single-Tie version (see page 164). After the Heel is turned (D), the shaped Foot is worked by increasing on one side only (E), then slipped onto dpns, with the remainder of Sock worked in-the-round. The Socks are totally reversible. However, for the purposes of the instructions, one side is labeled RS and the other side WS. You may wish to place a marker to denote the RS.

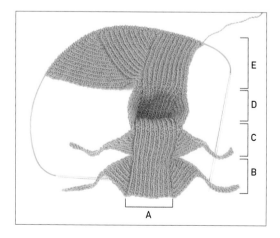

SOCKS

Notes: 1) Slip sts purlwise on odd numbered rows and knitwise on even numbered rows; 2) When knitting or purling a yo from a previous row, work it so that you close the hole (see Close the Yarnover, page 189).

ANKLES

Using circ needle, CO 21 sts.

Row 1 (WS): Slip 1, yo, [p1, k1] 9 times, p1, yo, p1–23 sts.

Row 2: Slip 1, p1, yo, [k1, p1] 9 times, k1, yo, p1, k1–25 sts.

Row 3: Slip 1, k1, p1, yo, [p1, k1] 9 times, p1, yo, p1, k1, p1–27 sts.

Row 4: Slip 1, p1, k1, p1, yo, [k1, p1] 9 times, k1, yo, [p1, k1] twice–29 sts.

Row 5: Slip 1, [k1, p1] twice, yo, [p1, k1] 9 times, p1, yo, [p1, k1] twice, p1–31 sts.

Row 6: Slip 1, [p1, k1] twice, p1, yo, [k1, p1] 9 times, k1, yo, [p1, k1] 3 times–33 sts.

Row 7: Slip 1, [k1, p1] 3 times, yo, [p1, k1] 9 times, p1, yo, [p1, k1] 3 times, p1–35 sts.

Row 8: Slip 1, [p1, k1] 3 times, p1, yo, [k1, p1] 9 times, k1, yo, [p1, k1] 4 times–37 sts.

Row 9: Slip 1, [k1, p1] 4 times, yo, [p1, k1] 9 times, p1, yo, [p1, k1] 4 times, p1–39 sts.

Row 10: Slip 1, [p1, k1] 4 times, p1, yo, [k1, p1] 9 times, k1, yo, [p1, k1] 5 times–41 sts.

Row 11: Slip 1, [k1, p1] 5 times, yo, [p1, k1] 9 times, p1, yo, [p1, k1] 5 times, p1–43 sts.

Row 12: Slip 1, [p1, k1] 5 times, p1, yo, [k1, p1] 9 times, k1, yo, [p1, k1] 6 times–45 sts.

Row 13: Slip 1, [k1, p1] 6 times, yo, [p1, k1] 9 times, p1, yo, [p1, k1] 6 times, p1–47 sts.

Row 14: Slip 1, [p1, k1] 6 times, p1, yo, [k1, p1] 9 times, k1, yo, [p1, k1] 7 times–49 sts.

Row 15: Slip 1, [k1, p1] 7 times, yo, [p1, k1] 9 times, p1, yo, [p1, k1] 7 times, p1–51 sts.

Next Row (RS): AO-f 16 sts at beginning of next row. BO 15 sts knitwise, slip last st back to left-hand needle, k2tog, starting with last st on right-hand needle BO 15 sts in rib pattern, [k1, p1] to last st, k1. *Note: If you wish to have longer ties, simply AO-f more than 16 sts, then BO 1 less st than you AO-f. Remember to repeat this when you work the tie on the opposite side.*

Next Row (WS): AO-f 16 sts at beginning of next row. BO 15 sts knitwise, yf, slip last st back to left-hand needle, p2tog, starting with last st on right-hand needle BO 15 sts in rib pattern, yo, [p1, k1] 9 times, p1, yo, p1.

TWO-TIE VERSION ONLY

Repeat from Row 2 once.

BOTH VERSIONS

Repeat Rows 2-15.

Work even for 4 rows, slipping first stitch of each row.

TURN HEEL

Next Row (RS): Slip 1, work 33 sts, ssk, *turn; slip 1 purlwise, work 17 sts, p2tog, turn; slip 1, work 17 sts, ssk; repeat from * 12 times–2 sts remain on left-hand needle. Do not turn; p1, k1, turn; slip 1, work to last 4 sts, p2tog, k1, p1–23 sts.

FOOT

Note: Slip sts knitwise on odd-numbered rows and purlwise on even-numbered rows.

Row 1 (RS): Slip 1, p1, yo, [k1, p1] 10 times, k1–24 sts.

Row 2: Slip 1, [k1, p1] 10 times, yo, p1, k1, p1–25 sts.

Row 3: Slip 1, [p1, k1] to yo, p1, yo, [k1, p1] 10 times, k1–26 sts.

Row 4: Slip 1, [k1, p1] 10 times, yo, [p1, k1] to last st, p1–27 sts.

Rows 5-8: Repeat Rows 3 and 4 twice–31 sts after Row 8.

Row 9: Slip 1, p1, yo, [k1, p1] 4 times, yo, [k1, p1] 10 times, k1–33 sts.

Row 10: Slip 1, [k1, p1] 10 times, yo, [p1, k1] 4 times, p1, yo, p1, k1, p1–35 sts.

Row 11: Slip 1, p1, [k1, p1] through yo, yo, [k1, p1] through yo, yo, [k1, p1] 10 times, k1–37 sts.

Row 12: Slip 1, [k1, p1] 10 times, yo, p1, [k1, p1] to yo, yo, p1, [k1, p1] to end–39 sts.

Rows 13-26: Repeat Rows 11 and 12 seven times–67 sts after Row 26.

Row 27: Slip 1, p1, [k1, p1] through yo, yo, [k1, p1] 10 times, k1, w&t; [p1, k1] 10 times, p1, yo, p1, [k1, p1] to end–69 sts.

Row 28: Slip 1, p1, [k1, p1] through yo, yo, [k1, p1] 8 times, k1, w&t; [p1, k1] 8 times, p1, yo, p1, [k1, p1] to end–71 sts.

Row 29: Slip 1, p1, [k1, p1] through yo, yo, [k1, p1] 6 times, k1, w&t; [p1, k1] 6 times, p1, yo, p1, [k1, p1] to end–73 sts.

Row 30: Slip 1, p1, [k1, p1] through yo, yo, [k1, p1] 4 times, k1, w&t; [p1, k1] 4 times, p1, yo, p1, [k1, p1] to end–75 sts.

Row 31: Slip 1, p1, [k1, p1] through yo, yo, [k1, p1] twice, k1, w&t; [p1, k1] 2 times, p1, yo, p1, [k1, p1] to end–77 sts.

Row 32: Slip 1, [p1, k1] 12 times, w&t; [p1, k1] to last st, p1.

Row 33: Slip 1, [p1, k1] 10 times, w&t; [p1, k1] to last st, p1.

Row 34: Slip 1, [p1, k1] 7 times, w&t; [p1, k1] to last st, p1.

Row 35: Slip 1, [p1, k1] 5 times, w&t; [p1, k1] to last st, p1.

Row 36: Slip 1, [p1, k1] twice, w&t; [p1, k1] to last st, p1.

Row 37: Hiding wraps as you go, slip 1, [p1, k1] to end.

JOIN FOOT

Divide sts onto 4 dpns as follows: With work in left hand, slip last 21 sts worked onto Needle 4, next 19 sts onto Needle 3, next 19 sts onto Needle 2, and last 18 sts onto Needle 1.

Note: Needles 1 and 2 hold sts for top of Foot; Needles 3 and 4 hold sts for bottom.

Rnd 1: Join for working in the rnd. Work in rib as established to last st, slip last st onto Needle 1.

Rnd 2: Ssk, work to end–76 sts remain.

Work even until piece measures 2" from join, or to 1¼" shorter than desired length from back of heel.

Rnd 3: Needles 1 and 2: Work even; Needle 3: K2tog, work to end of needle; Needle 4: Work to last 2 sts, k2tog–74 sts remain.

Rnd 4: Needle 1: Ssk, work to end of needle; Needle 2: Work to last 2 sts on needle, k2tog; Needle 3: Ssk, work to end of needle. Needle 4: Work to last 2 sts, k2tog–70 sts remain.

Repeat Rnd 4 eleven times–26 sts remain [13 sts on top, 13 sts on bottom].

Slip sts from Needle 2 onto Needle 1 and sts from Needle 4 onto Needle 3. Graft sts together using K1, P1 graft (see page 184).

Weave in ends.

one-run socks

This funky footwear is knit in one continuous run. No cutting, no reattaching, no extra ends to weave in other than the first tail from the cast-on and the last tail of the bind-off. The bands and arch, worked in Knit-Only Lace (page 38), provide textural contrast to the knit 1, purl 1 rib that runs down the back and along the sole of the sock. For an even more far-out look, you could add extra horizontal bands at the top to lengthen the sock into a modern-day version of the gladiator sandal.

LYNNE BARR

SIZES
Small (Large)

FINISHED MEASUREMENTS
7½" long from back of heel
6" foot circumference
Note: These Socks are extremely stretchy because of the stitch pattern and the elastic content of the yarn used, and should fit a very wide range of sizes. Try the Socks on as you go. If you are using a yarn without elastic and would like to adjust the width of the Leg or add length to the Foot, the instructions indicate where to do so.

YARN
Knit One Crochet Too Soxx Appeal (96% superwash merino wool / 3% nylon / 1% elastic; 208 yards / 50 grams): 2 balls #9419 Toffee

NEEDLES
One set of five double-pointed needles (dpn) size
US 3 (3.25 mm)
Change needle size if necessary to obtain correct gauge.

GAUGE
10 sts and 10 rows = 1" (2.5 cm) in K1, P1 Rib

STITCH PATTERNS
KNIT-ONLY LACE (see photo, page 38)
(multiple of 2 sts; 2-row repeat)
Row 1 (WS): *K1, k1-wy2; repeat from * to end.
Row 2: *Knit first wrap, dropping it from left-hand needle (see st instructions, page 38), insert tip of right-hand needle through remaining wrap purlwise, then into next st knitwise (without working wrap), pull st through wrap and knit it, drop wrap from left-hand needle (it will wrap loosely around st just knit); repeat from * to end.
Repeat Rows 1 and 2 for Knit-Only Lace.

KNIT-ONLY LACE IN-THE-RND
(multiple of 2 sts; 2-rnd repeat)
Rnd 1: *P1-wy2, p1; repeat from * to end.
Rnd 2: Work as for Row 2 of Knit-Only Lace.
Repeat Rnds 1 and 2 for Knit-Only Lace in-the-Rnd.

NOTES
The socks are totally reversible. However, for the purposes of the instructions, one side will be labeled RS and the other side WS.

SOCKS

Notes: 1) All yo's are worked as Beginning of Row Yarnovers (see page 189) to add-on sts at the sides (see photo 1). These sts will be worked later as Knit-Only Lace bands (see photo 2). 2) On Set-Up Row, a st remains on the left-hand needle, which will be treated as the first yo for that side of the Sock.

LEG

CO 19 sts.

Set-Up Row (WS): Yo(beg), [k1, p1] 9 times (1 st remains on left-hand needle), turn.

**Row 1: Yo(beg), [k1, p1] 9 times, turn; do not work yo at end of row.

Repeat Row 1 thirteen times–do not work yo's from previous rows.

There are 8 yo's on each side of the rib. Slip the 8 yo's on the side opposite the attached yarn onto a separate dpn (see photo 1). With an empty dpn, work the 8 yo's adjacent to the working yarn in Knit-Only Lace for 42 (46) rows [21 (23) repeats] (see photo 2). The band should measure approximately 5 (5½)" from rib. The rib and band should comfortably stretch to fit around leg, measured 6" up from ankle; if necessary, add or subtract one or more pattern repeats to make the rib and band fit comfortably. Knit 1 row.

Hold the needle with the band in front of and parallel to dpn with yo's, on opposite side of rib (see photo 3). To attach band to yo's, BO sts knitwise on both needles as follows: [K2tog (1 st from each needle)] twice, pso, *k2tog (1 st from each needle), pso, repeat from * 5 times. Place remaining st from BO onto needle with rib sts.

Row 2 (WS): K2tog, p1, [k1, p1] 8 times–18 sts remain.**
Repeat from ** to ** once, repeating Row 1 fifteen times instead of thirteen [8 yo's on each side of rib].

Row 3 (RS): Slip 1 knitwise, p1, [k1, p1] 8 times.
Row 4: Yo(beg), [k1, p1] 9 times.
Repeat Rows 3 and 4 seven times.
Row 5 (RS): Slip 1 knitwise, p1, [k1, p1] 8 times.

With an empty dpn, work the 8 yo's adjacent to the working yarn in Knit-Only Lace for 36 (38) rows [18 (19) repeats]. *Note: Add or subtract one or more pattern repeats if necessary to make the rib and band fit comfortably.* Work Row 1 of Knit-Only Lace once more. Hold needle with lace band next to the 18 sts of rib (see photo 4); with yarn attached to lace band, work across rib sts, attaching lace band to back of sock–26 sts (count double wraps as 1 st).

Row 6 (WS): Slip 1, p1, *[k1, p1] 8 times, work Row 2 of Knit-Only Lace over 8 sts.
Row 7: Yo(beg), work Row 1 of Knit-Only Lace over 8 sts, [k1, p1] 9 times.
Repeat Rows 6 and 7 seven times [8 yo's along lace side edge], then repeat Row 6 once (see photo 5).

With an empty dpn, work the 8 yo's in Knit-Only Lace for 29 rows, ending with Row 1 of pattern. *Note: Add or subtract one or more pattern repeats if necessary to make the rib and band fit comfortably.* Hold needle with lace band next to the 18 sts of rib (see photo 6); with yarn attached to lace band, work across rib sts, work Row 1 of Knit-Only Lace over last 8 sts–34 sts (count double wraps as 1 st). The 18 rib sts are now flanked by 8 lace sts on each side.

HEEL

Row 1 (RS): Yo(beg), work Row 2 of Knit-Only Lace over 8 sts, [k1, p1] 9 times, work Row 2 of Knit-Only Lace over 8 sts.
Row 2: Yo(beg), work Row 1 of Knit-Only Lace over 8 sts, [k1, p1] 9 times, work Row 1 of Knit-Only Lace over 8 sts.
Repeat Rows 1 and 2 eight (ten) times. Repeat Row 1 once more [9 (11) yo's on side with yarn attached, 10 (12) yo's on opposite side].
Next Row: Yo(beg), k8, ending row before rib sts [10 (12) yo's on each side]. Do not turn.

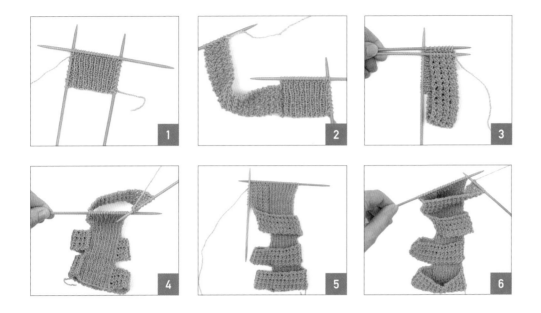

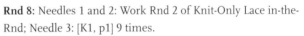

TURN HEEL

(WS) K1, *[p1, k1] 8 times, p2tog, turn; slip 1 knitwise; repeat from * 15 times, ending final repeat after working p2tog; do not turn and slip st–18 sts remain, with 10 (12) yo's on each side. Place yo's that are on the same dpn as the rib sts onto a separate dpn.

FOOT

Set-Up Row: Needle 1: With an empty dpn, [k1-tbl] 10 (12) times into yo's following the rib, CO 20 sts using Knitted CO (see page 178). Needle 2: Join for working in the rnd. With an empty dpn, k1-tbl 10 (12) times into yo's. Needle 3: With an empty dpn, [k1, p1] 9 times–58 (62) sts.

Rnds 1 and 3: Needles 1 and 2: *P1-wy2, p1; repeat from * to end of Needle 2; Needle 3: [K1, p1] 9 times.

Rnds 2 and 4: Needles 1 and 2: Work Rnd 2 of Knit-Only Lace in-the-Rnd; Needle 3: [K1, p1] 9 times. *Note: After Rnd 4 is worked the first time, slip 10 sts from Needle 1 to Needle 2 [20 (22) sts on each of the two needles].*

Rnd 5 (Decrease Rnd): Needles 1 and 2: P2tog, *p1-wy2, p1; repeat from * to last 2 sts on Needle 2, p2tog; Needle 3: [K1, p1] 9 times–56 (60) sts remain.

Rnd 6: Needles 1 and 2: K1, work Rnd 2 of Knit-Only Lace in-the-Rnd to last st on Needle 2, k1; Needle 3: [K1, p1] 9 times.

Rnd 7 (Decrease Rnd): Needles 1 and 2: P2tog-wy2, p1, *p1-wy2, p1; repeat from * to last 2 sts on Needle 2, p2tog; Needle 3: [K1, p1] 9 times–54 (58) sts remain.

Rnd 8: Needles 1 and 2: Work Rnd 2 of Knit-Only Lace in-the-Rnd; Needle 3: [K1, p1] 9 times.

Repeat Rnds 1-8 twice–46 (50) sts remain [14 (16) sts on Needles 1 and 2; 18 sts on Needle 3].

Repeat Rnds 1 and 2 until Foot measures 7½ (8¼)" from back of heel, or to desired Foot length, ending with Rnd 2.

Shape Toe

Repeat Rnds 5-8 three (four) times–34 sts remain [8 sts on Needles 1 and 2; 18 sts on Needle 3].

Turn to work Needle 3, slip 1, [p1, k1] 8 times, slip 1 from Needle 2 onto Needle 3, p2tog, turn; slip 1 knitwise, [p1, k1] 8 times, slip 1 from Needle 1 onto Needle 3, p2tog, turn–32 sts remain [7 sts on Needles 1 and 2; 18 sts on Needle 3].

Slip sts from Needle 2 onto Needle 1. Slip 1 st from each side of Needle 3 onto Needle 1 [16 sts on each needle]. Hold both needles together and graft using Kitchener st (see page 183).

Weave in ends.

linking hip sash

The links of this sash, with their modern Deco-like feel, are knit continuously into a chain with a scalloped lower edge. The blend of modern and ornate allows the sash to adorn both frilly and simple outfits. Because the sash is knit from the top down, short rows were added to a modified Looping Rib stitch (see page 32) to assure a downward drape. A single-link version is shown at right; a double-link version is shown on page 172.

FINISHED MEASUREMENTS

Single Linked Sash: 3" wide x 34" long, excluding Ties
Double Linked Sash: 4½" wide x 34" long, excluding Ties
Note: Sashes can be shortened or lengthened in 1½" increments. If you lengthen the sash beyond 36", you will need to purchase another hank of yarn.

YARN

Alchemy Bamboo (100% bamboo; 138 yards / 50 grams): Single Linked Sash: 1 hank #65E Dragon; Double Linked Sash: 2 hanks #37E Twig

NEEDLES

One 24" (60 cm) long or longer circular (circ) needle size US 4 (3.5 mm)
One set of three short double-pointed needles (dpn) size US 4 (3.5 mm)
Change needle size if necessary to obtain correct gauge.

NOTIONS

Stitch markers; stitch holder; 18 locking ring markers, to use as stitch holders *Note: If you add to the length, you will need an additional st holder for every 1½" you add.*

SASH

Notes: 1) Yo's along the side of the Sash Link Strap are not knit (see Beginning of Row Yarnovers, page 189). 2) Wind yarn into a ball that can be worked from both the outside and inside at the same time for the Single Linked Sash. 3) To lengthen or shorten the Sash, add or subtract yo's in groups of 6. Each group of 6 yo's adds approximately 1½" in length.

FIRST TIE

With dpns, CO 6 sts.
Next Row: Slip 1 knitwise, p1, [k1, p1] twice. Work even until piece measures 7" from the beginning.
Next Row: Slip 1, p1, AO-h 2 sts, k1, p1, AO-h 2 sts, k1, p1—10 sts.
Next Row: Slip 1 knitwise, p1, [k1, p1] 4 times. Work even for 5 rows.

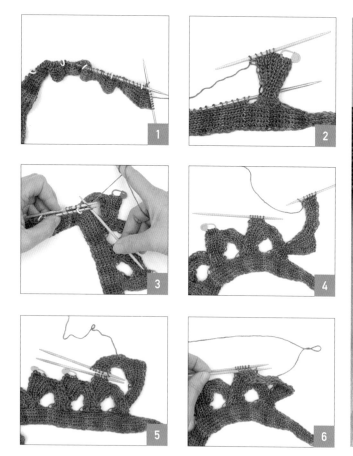

SASH LINK STRAP

Next Row: Change to circ needle. Continue to work rib for Sash Link Strap, but at the beginning of every other row, work yo (see Beginning of Row Yarnovers, page 189), until there are 108 yo's along one edge of the Tie. To keep track of the yo count, place a st marker after each 12 yo's (see photo 1). End rib at yo edge. Slip 10 sts of Tie onto st holder and leave yarn attached.

SASH LINKS

Notes: 1) Yo's in the Sash Links are increases and should be worked on the following row to close holes (see Close the Yarnover, page 189). 2) Pull yarn from center of ball for Single Linked Sash and work from second ball for Double Linked Sash. 3) Remove yo markers as you come to them.

Change to dpns, attach new strand of yarn and begin at end with finished Tie.

*Slip 1, p1, [k1, p1] twice, turn; repeat from * twice;
**yo, [k1, p1] 3 times, turn;
slip 1, p1, [k1, p1] twice, yo, p1, turn; slip 1, p1, yo, [k1, p1] 3 times, turn;
slip 1, p1, [k1, p1] twice, yo, p1, k1, p1, turn; slip 1, p1, k1, p1, yo, [k1, p1] 3 times, turn;
slip 1, p1, [k1, p1] twice, yo, p1, [k1, p1] twice, turn; *slip 1, p1, [k1, p1] 5 times; repeat from * 4 times, turn–12 sts.

SINGLE LINKED SASH ONLY

BO 5 sts in pattern, slip last st back to left-hand needle knitwise, k2tog, p1, [k1, p1] twice–6 sts remain.

DOUBLE LINKED SASH ONLY

Slip 1, p1, [k1, p1] 5 times. Slip 6 sts from end of dpn opposite attached yarn to st holder (see photo 2).

BOTH VERSIONS

*Slip 1, p1, [k1, p1] twice, turn; slip 1, p1, k1, p1, w&t;
[k1, p1] twice, turn; slip 1, p1, w&t;
k1, p1, turn; slip 1, p1, [k1, p1] twice, hiding wraps as you come to them, turn;
Slip 1, p1, [k1, p1] twice, turn; slip 1, p1, k1, w&t;
p1, k1, p1, turn; slip 1, p1, [k1, p1] twice, hiding wrap as you come to it; repeat from * once.

Rotate dpn counterclockwise and hold in back of next 6 yo's on circ needle, [k2tog (1 st from each needle), p2tog (1 st from each needle)] 3 times (see Photo 3).

*Slip 1, p1, [k1, p1] twice, turn; repeat from * once.

Repeat from ** until 6 yo's remain on circ needle.

You can now wrap either version of the Sash around your hips to see if the length is correct. The finished Sash will stretch a bit, so put some tension on it now as you check the length. If you need to lengthen the Sash, slip the 10 Tie sts back onto a needle and work more Sash Link Strap in 6 yo increments. If you lengthen the Sash, work more Sash Links until 6 yo's remain on circ needle.

SINGLE LINKED SASH ONLY

Break yarn attached to Sash Link sts on dpn, leaving a 7" tail.
Rotate dpn counterclockwise and hold in back of last 6 yo's on circ needle. Graft sts on dpn and circ needle together using K1, P1 graft (see page 183).

DOUBLE LINKED SASH ONLY

Rotate dpn counterclockwise and hold in back of last 6 yo's on circ needle; [k2tog (1 st from each needle), p2tog (1 st from each needle)] 3 times.

*Slip 1, p1, [k1, p1] twice; repeat from * 11 times.

***Yo, [k1, p1] 3 times, turn; slip 1, p1, [k1, p1] twice, yo, p1, turn;
slip 1, p1, yo, [k1, p1] 3 times, turn; slip 1, p1, [k1, p1] twice, yo, p1, k1, p1, turn;
slip 1, p1, k1, p1, yo, [k1, p1] 3 times, turn; slip 1, p1, [k1, p1] twice, yo, p1, [k1, p1] twice, turn;
*slip 1, p1, [k1, p1] 5 times, turn; repeat from * 5 times–12 sts.

BO 5 sts in pattern, slip last st back to left-hand needle knitwise, k2tog, p1, [k1, p1] twice–6 sts remain.

Slip 1, p1, [k1, p1] twice, turn; slip 1, p1, k1, p1, w&t;
[k1, p1] twice, turn; slip 1, p1, w&t;
k1, p1, turn; slip 1, p1, [k1, p1] twice, hiding wraps as you come to them, turn;
slip 1, p1, [k1, p1] twice, turn; slip 1, p1, k1, w&t;
p1, k1, p1, turn; slip 1, p1, [k1, p1] twice, hiding wrap as you come to it, turn;
slip 1, p1, [k1, p1] twice. Do not turn.

To attach Sash Link to next 6 sts on hold, slip sts from holder to dpn (see photo 4). Rotate working needle counterclockwise (see photo 5) to hold in front of next 6 sts on dpn (see photo 6). Hold both needles together and [k2tog (1 st from each needle, p2tog (1 st from each needle)] 3 times. Repeat from *** until last 6 sts on hold remain.

Slip last 6 sts onto a dpn. Rotate working needle to hold parallel to last 6 sts and graft sts together using K1, P1 graft.

BOTH VERSIONS

Finish Second Tie

Slip 10 sts from holder back onto dpn.
Slip 1 knitwise, k2tog, [p1, k1] 3 times, p1–9 sts remain.
Slip 1 knitwise, k2tog, [p1, k1] twice, p2–8 sts remain.
Slip 1 knitwise, p2tog, [k1, p1] 2 times, p1–7 sts remain.
Slip 1 knitwise, p2tog, [k1, p1] twice–6 sts remain.
Slip 1, p1, [k1, p1] twice. Work even for 7".
BO all sts in pattern.

Weave in ends. Lightly press Sash with iron and a damp cloth. If needed, stretch slightly so Sash Links lie flat.

Special Techniques

Special Techniques

ADD-ON STITCHES

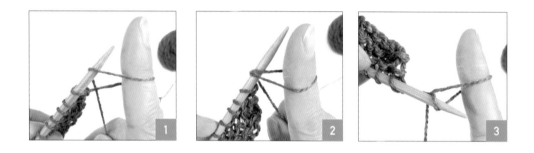

This is a method of adding on stitches to a work already in progress–either at the beginning or in the middle of a row.

Stitches can be added on with either a full twist (AO-f), or a half twist (AO-h). The half twist uses less yarn, which makes it the ideal choice for the Two-Tone Vest, where two stitches are inserted at once within a rib–using less yarn makes the double increase less obvious. The full twist Add-On is used when you desire a sturdier base for the stitches.

Add-On Half Twist (AO-h)

Note: This is also known as Backward Loop, Half-Hitch, or E-Wrap CO. To add on at the beginning of a row, hold working needle in your left hand. Twist yarn clockwise around right index finger, and insert left needle tip upward into the loop =(see photo 1). Pull the yarn so the new stitch is snug against its neighbor, but not so tight on the needle that you are unable to knit the stitch.

To add on in the middle of a row, keep working needle in your right hand. Twist yarn counterclockwise around left index finger, and insert working needle tip upward into the loop. Pull the yarn so the new stitch is snug against its neighbor, but not so tight on the needle that you are unable to knit the stitch.

Add-On Full Twist (AO-f)

To add on at the beginning of a row, hold working needle in your left hand. Twist yarn clockwise around right index finger, and with left-hand needle, reach backward under both strands of the loop (see photo 2), and insert tip downward into the loop (see photo 3). Pull the yarn so the new stitch is snug against its neighbor, but not so tight on the needle that you are unable to knit the stitch.

To add on in the middle of a row, keep working needle in your right hand. Twist yarn counterclockwise around left index finger, and with working needle reach backward under both strands of the loop, and insert needle downward into the loop. Pull the yarn so the new stitch is snug against its neighbor, but not so tight on the needle that you are unable to knit the stitch.

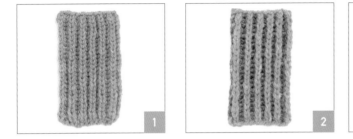
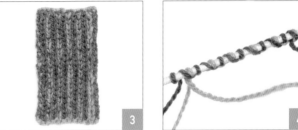

Brioche is a reversible pattern that looks somewhat similar to a K1, P1 Rib when knit in a solid color (see photo 1). When worked in two colors, the knitting looks different on opposite sides as each color assumes a dominant position where its knit columns protrude, and alternate columns recede. The main color (MC) (the color used to cast on) appears as dominant knit columns, with the contrasting color (CC) receding in photo 2. In photo 3 the CC appears as dominant columns with the MC receding.

In a simplified description, the basis for both solid and two-color brioches is "slip 1, yo, k2tog (or p2tog)." Each "slip 1, yo" is considered a pair and will always be the two stitches that are k2tog (or p2tog) on subsequent rows. See photo 4 for a close-up of the "slip 1, yo" pairs alternating with the solitary stitches that result from a k2tog (or p2tog).

In the headband pattern by Nancy Marchant (see page 135), you will see the abbreviations brk1 (brioche knit 1) and brp1 (brioche purl 1), originated by Nancy to represent k2tog and p2tog specifically for brioche. I have included both abbreviations, since they seem to appear equally in available patterns. For comprehensive information and techniques about brioche, I suggest you visit Nancy's website–www.briochestitch.com.

K2tog (or Brk1)

When working a k2tog, always knit together the "slip 1, yo" pair from the previous row.

The yarnover prior to the k2tog is made by beginning with the yarn in front, and carrying the yarn over the right-hand needle to make the k2tog. The yarnover and k2tog become one continuous action, with the k2tog beginning first if you insert the right-hand needle into the pair before the yarn is taken over the right-hand needle to make the yarnover. After the k2tog, the previous slipped stitch now has a yarnover across it.

P2tog (or Brp1)

To p2tog, always purl together the "slip 1, yo" pair from the previous row.

To yarnover before a p2tog, wrap the yarn counterclockwise around the right-hand needle once, ending in front. There is now a yarnover across the previous slipped stitch.

Solid-Color Brioche

Solid-color brioche is a simple one-row pattern, in which every other stitch is slipped purlwise with a yarnover crossing from front to back over the slipped stitch. On the same row, all the "slip 1, yo" pairs from the previous row are worked as k2tog. Prior to the first pattern row is a setup row to create the first set of "slip 1, yo" pairs.

Solid-Color Brioche Pattern

Note: The pattern will clearly emerge when you have worked approximately one inch in length.
Loosely CO an even number of stitches.
Set-Up Row: *Slip 1 wyif, yo, k1; repeat from * to end.
Row 1: *Slip 1 wyif, yo, k2tog; repeat from * to end.
Repeat Row 1 for Solid-Color Brioche Pattern.

Two-Color Brioche

Always work on circular or double-pointed needles to allow two passes to be worked for each row–one pass for each color. After the first pass is worked with the first color, slide all stitches back to the opposite end of the needle in order to work the second color for that row.

Two-Color Brioche Pattern

Using double-pointed needles (dpn) or a circular (circ) needle, with MC, loosely CO an even number of sts.

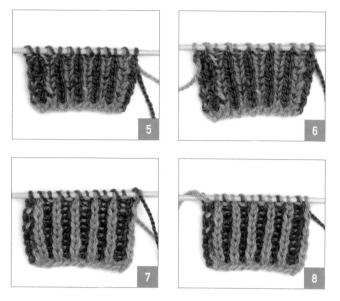

Set-Up Row CC: Slide CO sts to opposite end of needle and join CC. *Slip 1 wyif, yo, p1; repeat from * to end (see photo 4 – green is MC, blue is CC).

Row 1 MC: *Slip 1 wyif, yo, p2tog; repeat from * to end. Do not turn work.

Row 1 CC: Slide work to opposite end of needle. *K2tog, slip 1 wyif, yo; repeat from * to end. Turn work.

Row 2 MC: *Note: On the first k2tog of the row, be sure to include the last yo from the previous row.* *K2tog, slip 1 wyif, yo; repeat from * to end. Do not turn work.

Row 2 CC: Slide work to opposite end of needle. *Slip 1 wyif, yo, p2tog; repeat from * to end. *Note: On the final p2tog, be sure to include the MC yo from the previous row.*

Repeat Rows 1 and 2, MC and CC, for Two-Color Brioche Pattern.

Some Rules to Consider

Once you have followed the directions above for several rows and the knitting on your needles clearly shows the pattern, you could continue without referring to the written directions if you keep the following five rules in mind.

Rule 1

The cast-on color is the MC; always work the MC first. So if your yarns are on opposite ends of the needle, the next yarn to work with is CC because it always follows MC and has to catch up.

Rule 2

Within a row, stitches to be slipped are always alone, and want to be covered by yarnovers to create pairs. The stitches that will be knit together or purled together are already paired with yarnovers.

Rule 3

When a single stitch is slipped, always slip it with the yarn in front. That includes the first stitch–there are no exceptions.

Rule 4

Pairs at the top of receding columns are always worked as p2tog. Pairs atop dominant columns are always worked as k2tog.

Rule 5

Yarnovers are always made after a stitch is slipped. Even when it's the last stitch of the row that is slipped, you still yarnover. Whether you work the next pair p2tog or k2tog (see Rule 4) determines what kind of yarnover to make. Before a p2tog, completely circle the right needle once to make your yarnover. Before a k2tog, simply yarnover across the top of the right needle as you work the k2tog.

How to Interpret Rows Following the Five Rules

In photos 5-8, the cast-on color is green, therefore MC is green and CC is blue.

Photo 5

Rule 1: Since both yarns are on the same side, work with MC.

Rules 2 and 3: The first stitch is alone, so it will be slipped, keeping MC to the front.

Rules 4 and 5: The next pair is at the top of a receding column, so yarnover once around the right needle, then p2tog.

Photo 6

Rule 1: Since yarns are on opposite sides, work with CC.

Rule 2: The row begins with a pair that is at the top of a dominant column, so k2tog.

Rule 3: The next stitch is alone, so it will be slipped, keeping CC to the front.

Rules 4 and 5: The next pair is at the top of a dominant column, so yarnover the top of the right needle as you k2tog.

Photo 7

Rule 1: Since both yarns are on the same side, work with MC.

Rule 2: The row begins with a pair that is at the top of a dominant column, so k2tog.

Rule 3: The next stitch is alone, so it will be slipped, keeping MC to the front.

Rules 4 and 5: The next pair is at the top of a dominant column, so yarnover the top of the right needle as you k2tog.

Photo 8

Rule 1: Since yarns are on opposite sides, work with CC.

Rules 2 and 3: The first stitch is alone, so it will be slipped, keeping CC to the front.

Rules 4 and 5: The next pair is at the top of a receding column, so yarnover once around the right needle, then p2tog.

The execution of this cast-on is similar to a long-tail cast-on, but it's not identical. It alternates stitches with two different color yarns, but does not interlock them, which makes it perfect for starting open-ended tubes in two colors (see Two-Color Tube, page 182). For interlocked double knits, use the Tubular Two-Color Cast-On (see page 180) that interlocks the two colors during the cast-on and has a rounded invisible edge.

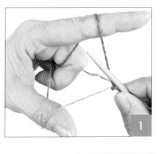

Step 1: Loosely tie together the ends of two different color yarns, leaving tails long enough to weave in later. Hold the loose knot below a needle in your right hand and drape the two colors over your thumb and index finger, with yarns held secure by your remaining fingers, just as you would for a long-tail cast-on in one color. (See photo 1, viewed from above, and photo 2, viewed from the front.)

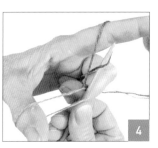

Step 2: Insert the tip of the needle upward through the loop around your thumb (see photo 3).

Step 3: With the tip of the needle, reach to the right past both strands of the color looped around your index finger, and insert the needle up through that loop (see photo 4). Do not insert needle downward through loop as you would with a long-tail cast-on.

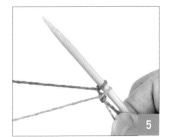

Step 4: Release both yarns, and pull to tighten around the needle (see photo 5).

Again, drape both yarns over your thumb and index finger, keeping the two colors in the same positions as before. Repeat Steps 2-4 for desired number of stitches. Viewed from the bottom, the cast-on looks like a column of knitting with one side of the stitch in one color and the other side of the stitch in the second color (see photo 6).

Any time after you have one inch of knitting completed, undo the loose knot from the cast-on and weave in the tails.

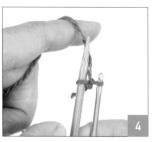

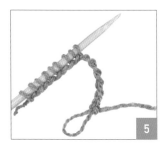
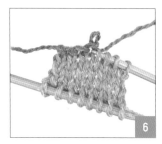

Both Knitted Cast-On and Cable Cast-On are worked similarly, however, the Cable Cast-On, which is made by knitting between stitches, is sturdier with less stretch than the Knitted Cast-On, which makes a new stitch by knitting into a single stitch.

Knitted Cast-On

Step 1: Make a slipknot and place it on your needle.

Step 2: Knit into the slipknot and place the new stitch on the left-hand needle (see photo 1).

Step 3: Knit into the last stitch (see photo 2) and place the new stitch on the left-hand needle. Repeat Step 3 until you have the desired number of stitches, including the initial slipknot in your count.

Cable Cast-On

Steps 1 and 2: Work Steps 1-2 as for Knitted Cast-On.

Step 3: Insert right-hand needle between last two stitches (see photo 3), draw up a loop, and place loop onto left-hand needle. Repeat Step 3 to continue making new stitches. To keep the stitches uniform, I use my thumb as a spacer when placing a new stitch on the needle, until the loop has been tightened.

If you are using either of these cast-ons to add stitches onto a work in progress, work only Step 3 until you have cast on the number of stitches that are specified in the pattern.

A provisional cast-on allows for a temporary set of stitches to be used to begin your knitting, which will be removed later. These stitches are cast on with scrap yarn that will later be removed and discarded. The best scrap yarn to use is smooth, easy to pull out and slightly finer than the yarn to be used for your project.

There are different methods for working a provisional cast-on. With the methods I tried, the results for each were the same, but the one that I found quick and foolproof every time was to crochet stitches directly onto a knitting needle.

The single problem I found when removing the provisional cast-on from the methods I tried occurred when I removed the cast-on to place stitches on a needle. The first edge stitch always disappeared once it was released from the provisional yarn.

The way I resolved to fix the problem was to cast on one more stitch than required by my project and then k2tog at the problem edge on the first row of my knitting. This is written into the directions that follow.

Crochet Provisional Stitches onto a Knitting Needle

With scrap yarn, make a slipknot and insert a crochet hook into the loop.

Step 1: Hold the crochet hook to the right of a vertically held knitting needle, with the working scrap yarn behind the knitting needle (see photo 1).

Step 2: Reach with the crochet hook across the front of the knitting needle and grab the yarn (see photo 2).

Step 3: Pull the yarn through the loop on the crochet hook (see photo 3).

Step 4: Move the yarn over the tip of the knitting needle to the back (see photo 4).

Repeat Steps 1-4 until you have one more stitch on the knitting needle than is required for your project. This extra stitch is necessary to avoid losing a stitch when the scrap yarn is later removed.

Work a crochet chain of six more stiches free of the knitting needle; cut yarn, leaving approximately 3" to make a slipknot that will easily pull out later (see photo 5).

With your project yarn, either knit all stitches or purl all stitches for one row before starting your project. If you knit the first row, then k2tog at the side edge where the crochet tail is to eliminate the extra stitch from the cast-on. If you purled the first row, then p2tog. This locks in the edge stitch from the provisional cast-on. Do not begin working a rib or a pattern of mixed stitches immediately after the cast-on or the scrap yarn crochet will not pull away freely when you later try to remove it.

Remove Scrap Yarn

Pull the slipknot from the end of the crochet chain, and continue pulling until you reach the interlocked crochet and project stitches. Now work slowly and slip each project stitch onto a needle as it is released from the crochet chain (see photo 6).

Combining Stitches is a way of working stitches from two needles onto one. When used in conjunction with dividing stitches (see Divide Stitches, page 185), it produces three-dimensional shapes, such as those seen in the Fins and Cut Cables stitch patterns (see pages 48 and 52).

Combine Stitches into a K1, P1 Rib

Step 1: Hold two needles together in your left hand.

Step 2: K1 from the front needle.

Step 3: P1 from the back needle.

Alternate Steps 2 and 3 until you have combined all of the stitches (or number specified in pattern).

Combine Stitches into K2, P2 and K3, P3 Ribs

Needles are held in the same position as the K1, P1 version, except when combining into a K2, P2 Rib, you alternate k2 from one needle and p2 from the other. Similarly, you alternate k3 and p3 when combining into a K3, P3 Rib.

Combine Stockinette Stitch

You can also combine two needles onto one needle in Stockinette stitch. Hold both needles in your left hand with the knit sides facing you, and alternate knitting one stitch from each needle. For Reverse Stockinette st, hold purl sides facing you, and alternate purling one stitch from each needle as in Cut Cables (page 52).

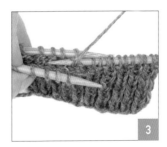

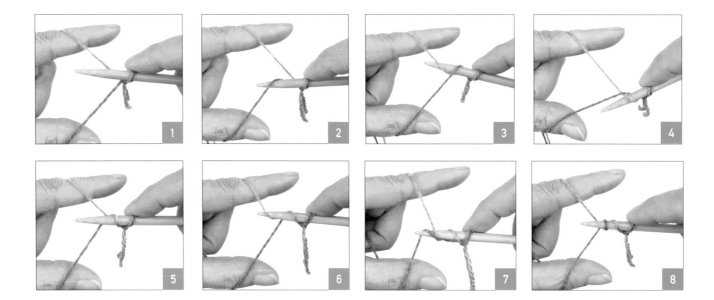

The Tubular Two-Color Cast-On is perfect for double knitting when there are different colors on opposite sides beginning on the first row. This applies to Véronik Avery's Lice Jacket (see page 150), and it is the cast-on that she specifies using in her pattern.

Step 1: With colors A and B held together, make a slipknot, leaving a 4" tail in each color, and place slipknot on your needle. Drape color B over your thumb and color A over your forefinger (see photo 1; A is aqua, B is brown).

Step 2: Bring the tip of the needle toward you over the top of B (thumb yarn) then under it (see photo 2). Move the needle away from you over A (forefinger yarn), catching it (see photo 3); carry A under B (see photo 4), then bring the needle over B back to its centered starting position with a stitch in color A (see photo 5).

Step 3: Move the tip of the needle away from you, over then under A (see photo 6). Take the needle under, then over B, catching it (see photo 7). Bring the needle under A then over and back to the starting position with a new stitch in B (see photo 8).

Repeat Steps 2 and 3 until you have the desired number of stitches; do not include the slipknot in the stitch count. Hold the yarns secure so they don't untwist after the last stitch, until the first row is worked.

Work the first paired row as follows:
With A in back, slip 1 (color B), making sure the yarns are twisted at the beginning of the row so that you do not lose the first st, take A to the front under the right-hand needle, p1, *yb, slip 1 wyib, yf, p1; repeat from * to end. Drop the slipknot off the needle, but do not untie until after the second paired row (fourth pass) has been worked. Do not turn work; slide sts to opposite end of needle. With B, *yb, k1, yf, slip 1 wyif; repeat from * to end.

Double knitting (DK) is a method of knitting two Stockinette stitch fabrics simultaneously, with two separate balls of yarn and a single circular needle or two double-pointed needles. The two fabrics may be interlocked, and therefore inseparable, or they may be two separate, unconnected fabrics. Because the finished fabric is doubled, it will be heavier than a single thickness, but light to medium-weight fabrics can still be knit if a lace or sport-weight yarn is used.

In action, double knitting is just a K1, P1 Rib where the knit stitches create a design on one side and the purls create an inverted design or a completely different design on the other. With inverted patterns, both colors can be worked in the same row if stitches are worked as pairs, with two yarns of different colors carried together in a single pass. For this single-pass method, standard charts are used. If knitting a completely different design on each side, then separate passes for each color must be made for each row. For the double-pass method, you work from special DK charts.

In both cases, single-pass and double-pass, once the two sides are established using the k1, p1 pattern, they never vary. When you turn your work so the other side is facing you, just as with a K1, P1 Rib, what were knit stitches on the other side are now purls facing you, and the purls from the other side now appear as knit stitches.

Knitting Single-Pass DK from Standard Charts

Many knitters use a standard format chart for working double knit, such as the one for Véronik Avery's beautiful jacket (see page 150). These double-knit fabrics are the same design on both sides, with the colors inverted.

Since you are working two sides at once, you will need to cast on twice the number of stitches shown on the chart. The best cast-on to use is the Tubular Two-Color Cast-On (see page 180), which sets up the two different color sides from the start.

When working from standard charts, knitters carry both color yarns together across a row, alternating one stitch with the first color, followed by the next stitch with the second color. The stitches are always worked in pairs, with each stitch on the chart corresponding to a k1, p1 pair of stitches on the needles. The main color (MC) on the side that is shown on the chart will be

the contrasting color (CC) on the other side, and vice versa. On the side that is facing you, the knit stitches will be the MC for that side. So while following a standard chart, when you knit a stitch in the MC, purl the next stitch in the CC yarn. When you knit a stitch in the CC, purl the next stitch in the MC. And always carry both colors together from front to back and back to front, only separating them in order to k1 or p1 as you follow the pattern on the chart.

Reading a single-pass DK chart is a bit more complicated when working back and forth in rows, since you will have to reverse the colors with which you are working when you work opposite side rows. For example, when working Véronik's Back Medallion Chart, on all odd-numbered rows, you will work all the knit sts in A and all the purl sts in B. This is simple because it matches what you see when you're working. However, when working even-numbered rows, you will have to reverse the colors and work all the knit sts in B and all the purl sts in A, exactly the opposite of what you see in the chart. So when working Row 4 of the chart from left to right, for instance, you will knit the first st in A and purl the next stitch in B, the opposite of what is shown in the chart. You will find that this will only be a challenge for the first several rows of the chart, after which the pattern will become evident, and you will find it easy to switch the colors.

Knitting Double-Pass DK from DK Charts

To knit completely different designs on opposite sides, you will need to work two passes across the stitches for each row. This double-pass is not for working the two sides separately, but for working the two colors separately. To work the first pass, the contrasting color (CC) yarn is used to knit and purl the stitches for the patterns on both sides for that color. Then for the second pass, slide all stitches back to the opposite end of the needle, and with the main color (MC) yarn, knit and purl all remaining stitches that were not worked with the CC yarn. During each pass, the stitches that are not worked with the current yarn color will be slipped, with the working yarn carried in front of the slipped purl stitches and behind the slipped knit stitches.

You'll notice that DK charts are quite different from other charts. They have additional vertical gray columns that alternate between white columns. The white columns represent the A side, and the gray columns represent the B side.

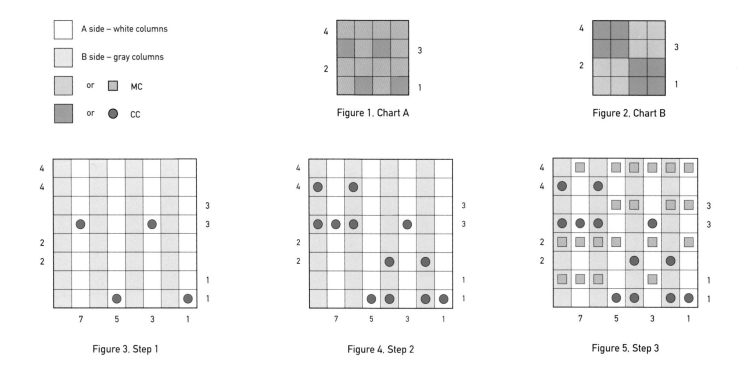

Figure 1. Chart A

Figure 2. Chart B

Figure 3. Step 1

Figure 4. Step 2

Figure 5. Step 3

The double-pass rows are indicated in the chart as paired row numbers that run up the left and right sides of the chart. As with standard charts, for all odd number pairs on the right side of chart, read the chart from right to left. For all even number pairs on the left side of chart, read the chart from left to right.

For all odd paired rows, following the chart from right to left, the A side sts are knit and the B side sts are purled. For all even paired rows, following the chart from left to right, the A side stitches are purled and the B side stitches are knit. For all stitches not worked on either pair of odd and even rows, the yarn is carried behind the slipped knit stitches and in front of the slipped purl stitches.

Converting Two Standard Charts into a DK Chart

For a simple example, standard format Charts A (see Figure 1) and B (see Figure 2) will be converted to a DK chart (see Figure 5). Chart A represents the pattern that you will see when looking at side A of the fabric. Chart B represents side B of the fabric.

Step 1: Transcribe CC stitches from Chart A onto white (side A) squares in DK Chart. CC stitches go in the lower row of each row pair (Figure 3).

Step 2: Transcribe CC stitches from Chart B onto gray (side B) squares in DK Chart. Again, CC stitches go in the lower row of each row pair. Now, both patterns from Charts A and B have been transcribed onto the DK Chart (Figure 4).

Step 3: To complete the DK chart, MC stitches need to be filled in on the upper row of each row pair. All squares above CC stitches will be left blank. All other squares must be filled in with the MC symbol (Figure 5). Again, side A stitches from Chart A will go in white squares and side B stitches from Chart B will go in gray squares. Note that when you have filled in all the appropriate squares, each row pair must have a stitch in each column, whether the stitch is in the first or the second row of the pair. Where there is a stitch in one column in the lower row of a pair, there will not be a stitch in the upper row, and vice versa. Only one stitch is permitted per column per row pair.

Separable Double Knit

This is double knitting that either separates into two pieces, or creates a tube if yarns are twisted at the edges (see Two-Color Tube below). For both results, two separate balls of yarn are used, and two passes are required for one row. Each ball will only be used to knit stitches on its own side, never crossing to the opposite side. If a yarn were used to work a stitch other than stitches from its own side, the two fabrics would end up joined at that point.

Two-Color Tube

Using a double-pointed needle (dpn) or circular (circ) needle, cast on an even number of stitches using the Double-Stitch Cast-On with Two Colors (see page 177).

Note: When working the following rows, sts on Pass 1 will be purled with the color of the second st on the left-hand needle, and sts on Pass 2 will be knit with the color of the first st on the left-hand needle.

Row 1 (work Pass 1 and Pass 2)

Pass 1: Slip 1, wrap yarn attached to next st on left-hand needle counterclockwise around the yarn attached to the slipped st, then bring it to the front between the needles, p1, *slip 1 wyib, p1; repeat from * to end. Slide work to opposite end of needle to work Pass 2 with next color.

Pass 2: *K1, slip1 wyib; repeat from * to end.

Repeat Row 1 (both passes) until tube is desired length. Divide sts, slipping knit sts to a front needle and purl sts to a back needle (see Divide Stitches, page 185). BO each side knitwise, wrapping yarn at edge of first bound-off side.

KITCHENER PLUS

Kitchener stitch, the commonly used method of grafting Stockinette stitch, need not be the only method in your repertoire of grafting stitches together. There are so many combinations of knit and purl patterns, and with four simple rules to help you understand the process of grafting, you can piece any of those combinations together. Understanding these rules will also liberate you from having to constantly reference instructions when working Kitchener stitch.

The following four rules apply when joining two pieces of the same design. Garter stitch is an exception to these rules and is explained separately on page 184.

Rule 1

To begin, hold the two pieces, on two separate needles, parallel together in your left hand with the same pattern of each piece facing each other. If the stitch facing you on the front needle is a knit stitch, then the stitch facing you on the back needle should be a purl stitch. For example, if the pattern facing you on the front needle is k1, p1, then the pattern facing you on the back needle is p1, k1.

Rule 2

There are only two simple moves, slip and lock. To slip, slip the next stitch off the needle with a threaded tapestry needle. To lock, run the tapestry needle through the next stitch on the needle, but do not slip the stitch off the needle. Always slip a stitch as it appears, and lock it in the direction opposite the stitch orientation. Specifically, knit stitches are slipped knitwise and purl stitches are slipped purlwise; knit stitches are locked purlwise and purl stitches are locked knitwise.

Rule 3

The stitches on both needles are always worked in pairs as a two-step process. For Step 1, the first stitch is slipped, and for Step 2, the second stitch is locked. Alternate working both needles with these two steps. So, slip the first stitch and lock the second stitch on the front needle, then slip and lock on the back needle. Repeat again and again until all stitches on both needles are grafted together.

Rule 4

Since the stitch patterns on both needles are the same, with the same sides facing each other, the back stitches are the inverse of the front stitches. That means you only have to read the stitches on the front needle to determine how to slip and lock, because the back needle will be worked in the reverse of the front needle. For example, if stitches on the front needle are worked "slip knitwise, lock purlwise," then the stitches on the back needle will be worked "slip purlwise, lock knitwise."

Optional First Stitch Locks

Note: Set-Up Steps 1 and 2 are optional, and you may wish to omit them if you prefer a softer, graded transition, as for sock toes.

Set-Up Step 1: To lock the first stitch on the front needle, run the TN through a knit stitch purlwise, or through a purl stitch knitwise.

Set-Up Step 2: To lock the first stitch on the back needle, run the TN through a knit stitch purlwise, or through a purl stitch knitwise.

Grafting Stockinette Stitch (Kitchener Stitch)

Cut the working yarn, leaving a tail four times the width of the pieces to be grafted, and thread it onto a tapestry needle (TN).

Hold the needles parallel to each other with purl sides facing each other. On the front needle, you have all knit stitches facing you, and on the back needle, all purl stitches facing you.

Step 1: With the TN, slip the first stitch knitwise off the front needle.

Step 2: To lock the next stitch on the front needle, run the TN through it purlwise and leave it on the needle.

Step 3: With the TN, slip the purl stitch purlwise off the back needle.

Step 4: To lock the next stitch on the back needle, run the TN through it knitwise and leave it on the needle.

Repeat Steps 1-4 until there is only one stitch left on each needle.

Then with the TN, slip the stitch off the front needle knitwise, and the stitch off the back needle purlwise. Secure the yarn and trim the tail.

Grafting K1, P1 Rib

Cut the working yarn, leaving a tail four times the width of the pieces to be grafted, and thread it onto a tapestry needle (TN).

Hold the needles parallel to each other with the same pattern facing each other. The front needle begins with k1, p1 facing you, and the back needle begins with p1, k1 facing you.

Step 1: With the TN, slip the first stitch knitwise off the front needle.

Step 2: To lock the next stitch on the front needle, run the TN through it knitwise and leave it on the needle.

Step 3: With the TN, slip the first stitch purlwise off the back needle.

Step 4: To lock the next stitch on the back needle, run the TN through it purlwise and leave it on the needle.

Step 5: With the TN, slip the next stitch off the front needle purlwise.

Step 6: To lock the next stitch on the front needle, run the TN through it purlwise and leave it on the needle.

Step 7: With the TN, slip the first stitch knitwise off the back needle.

Step 8: To lock the next stitch on the back needle, run the TN through it knitwise and leave it on the needle.

Repeat Steps 1-8 until there is only one stitch left on each needle. Then with the TN, slip the stitch off the front needle knitwise if it is a knit stitch, or purlwise if it is a purl stitch, and the stitch off the back needle purlwise if it is a purl stitch, or knitwise if it is a knit stitch. Secure the yarn and trim the tail.

Grafting Garter Stitch

The slip and lock, knitwise and purlwise rules are different for Garter stitch. When you graft, you are actually adding another row to each piece you are grafting and Garter stitch alternates knit rows and purl rows. Therefore when grafting Garter stitch, you want to work a row of stitches that is the opposite of the last row below the needles. If the last row of stitches facing you on both needles is knit, you will want to graft a purl row, so slip all stitches purlwise and lock all stitches knitwise. If the last row of

stitches facing you on both needles is purl, you will want to graft a knit row, so slip all stitches knitwise and lock all stitches purlwise.

For the following example, hold both needles parallel, with purl stitches on the last row of both needles facing you. Note that Steps 1 and 2 are worked the same for the front needles as Steps 3 and 4 are for the back needles, because all stitches facing you on both needles are purl stitches.

Cut the working yarn, leaving a tail four times the width of the pieces to be grafted, and thread it onto a tapestry needle (TN).

Step 1: With the TN, slip the first stitch knitwise off the front needle.

Step 2: To lock the next stitch on the front needle, run the TN through it purlwise and leave in on the needle.

Step 3: With the TN, slip the first stitch knitwise off the back needle.

Step 4: To lock the next stitch on the back needle, run the TN through it purlwise and leave it on the needle.

Repeat Steps 1-4 until there is only one stitch left on each needle. Then with the TN, slip the stitch off front needle knitwise, and the stitch off back needle knitwise. Secure yarn, and trim tail.

If the stitches facing you on both needles were knit stitches, then you would slip all stitches purlwise and lock all stitches knitwise on both needles.

K1, P1 Bind-Off with Kitchener

The method of binding off a K1, P1 Rib using the Kitchener stitch is the same as the method used to graft pieces together after you divide your knitting onto two separate needles, slipping knit stitches to a front needle and purl stitches to a back needle (see Divide Stitches, page 185).

Once your rib has been divided onto separate needles, notice that the stitch pattern on each needle is no longer k1, p1. Rather they are all knit stitches facing you on the front needle and all purl stitches facing you on the back needle. Therefore, the pieces can be joined following the steps above for Grafting Stockinette Stitch (Kitchener Stitch). Do not pull the yarn too tightly with this bind-off, as the edge should be able to stretch with the rib. However, if you are using this as a bind-off for double knitting, then you do not want to bind off loosely.

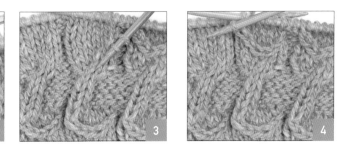

These stitches are picked up with a decorative purpose rather than a functional one. They can be used to create folds like those in Folded Fabric (see page 75), or to apply decorative patterns to a knit surface like Pick-Up Overlay (see page 66). They may also be used to create a base of stitches to build on three-dimensionally as in Checks and Flaps (see page 64).

When stitches are picked up in groups, and not knit as they are picked up, it is best to use a spare double-pointed needle (dpn) that is smaller than the needles being used for the project. The smaller needle size minimizes disturbance to adjacent stitches and to the base stitch from which the pick-up is being made. If pick-ups are knit immediately as they are picked up, then just use the narrow tip of the needle to pick up.

Pick-ups can be made from either a knit or purl stitch. When made from a purl, insert the pick-up dpn vertically from above or below a purl bump (see photo 1). Make pick-ups from a knit by inserting the pick-up dpn horizontally into either the left half (see photo 2) or right half of a knit stitch.

Using Pick-Ups to Draw Patterns
Pick up a stitch with an empty needle and knit the stitch. Pick up and knit another adjacent stitch. Once you have two stitches on your needle, bind off the previous stitch. You can continue to pick up, knit, and bind off stitches to create knit chain patterns on either the Stockinette or Reverse Stockinette side of your knitting. This method of decoration was used in J Cables (see page 68) to create the curved shapes (see photos 3 and 4).

Dividing stitches is a way of separating the knits and purls of a ribbed fabric onto two different needles to work them separately. In the stitch patterns that appear in this book, such as Puffy or Tucks and Cables (see page 56 or 58), stitches are separated to facilitate working two completely different patterns on opposing sides.

Divide a K1, P1 Rib
Hold knitting in your left hand and 2 empty needles parallel in your right hand.

Step 1: Slip next knit stitch onto the front needle (see photo 1).

Step 2: Slip next purl stitch onto the back needle (see photo 2). Repeat Steps 1 and 2.

Divide K2, P2 or K3, P3 Ribs
Hold working needle with stitches and empty needles in the same way as for K1, P1 Rib. Slip knit stitches to the front needle and purl stitches to the back needle in the order that you encounter them.

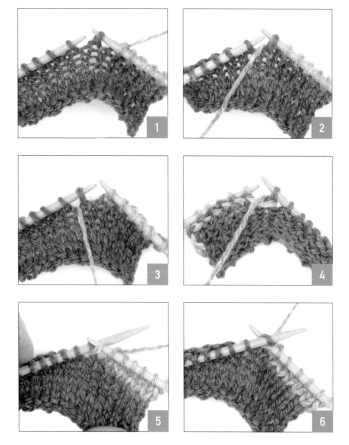

Short rows are a technique to work partial rows without leaving holes in your knitting.

Working Short Rows in Stockinette Stitch

The following directions are for short rows being worked on a knit row. Work them the same on purl rows, except substitute "knit side" for "purl side" in Step 4.

In pattern directions, these four steps are referred to as "w&t", an abbreviation for wrap and turn.

First, work up to the place where you will begin your short row. This place will be specified in your pattern, where you will most likely be instructed to work a certain number of stitches, then wrap and turn.

Step 1: With the yarn in back, slip the next stitch purlwise (see photo 1).

Step 2: Bring the yarn between the needles to the front (see photo 2).

Step 3: Slip the same stitch back to the left-hand needle (see photo 3).

Step 4: Turn the work and bring the yarn to the purl side between the needles (see photo 4).

Hiding Wraps from Stockinette Stitch Short Rows

On the first row after working a short row, if you will be working past the wrapped stitch (rather than working another short row before you get to the wrapped stitch), you will need to hide the wrap from the short-row shaping.

On a Knit Row: To hide a wrap, insert right-hand needle under wrap. Knit wrap and wrapped stitch together (see photos 5 and 6).

On a Purl Row: Pick up wrap and place it on left-hand needle. Purl wrap and wrapped stitch together.

Working Short Rows in Garter Stitch

Work Steps 1-3 as for Working Short Rows in Stockinette Stitch. When you turn your work, do not bring yarn back through needles in Step 4. Leave yarn to back to begin knitting.

Hiding Wraps from Garter Stitch Short Rows

Hide them the same as for knit row wraps (see photos 5 and 6). Occasionally when you work short rows in Garter stitch, it is best not to hide the wraps. It depends on the yarn being used. You may notice in some patterns in this book that you are instructed to hide wraps, and in others, you are not instructed to.

Short-Rowed Yarnovers

All the yarnovers, wrapped in short rows in this book, are slipped without twisting. If you slip the yarnover by catching the leading yarn of the yarnover loop you will not twist it. When working a wrapped yarnover, do not hide the wrap; instead, let the wrap remain wrapped around the yarnover.

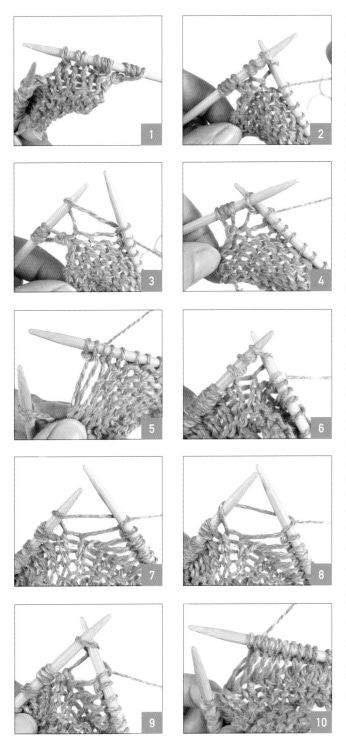

Wraps are made while knitting or purling a stitch. With a single wrap, you get the ordinary knit or purl stitches, but a varying number of wraps renders some very different looks. Most commonly seen are multiple wraps where the extra wraps are dropped on the following row, creating extra-long stitches. When you combine increases with varying multiple wraps, the result is a stitch pattern like Surf (see page 27) or Garter Triangles (see page 72).

Multiple Wraps

The abbreviations for multiple wraps are written as k1-wy2, k1-wy3 and k1-wy4 (or p1-wy2, p1-wy3, and p1-wy4 for purled sts). The "wy" stands for "wrap yarn", and the number following it indicates how many times to wrap the yarn around the right-hand needle while knitting (or purling) a stitch. From left to right in photo 1, the stitches on the right-hand needle are the result of k1, k1-wy2, k1-wy3, and k1-wy4.

Knitting the Wrapped Stitch

On the row after making a multiple wrap, knit into the leading wrap and allow the remaining wraps to drop from the left-hand needle to make a simple elongated stitch.

Increasing in Wrapped Stitches

Abbreviated as kw-f/b, this increase applies to all (k1-wy2, k1-wy3, or k1-wy4) wrapped stitches. It is equivalent to a k1-f/b and makes a single-stitch increase. Also like k1-f/b, this increase looks like a knit followed by a purl (see photo 5). The increase is made by knitting into the leading wrap (see photo 2), dropping wraps up to the last wrap (see photo 3), then knitting into the back of the last wrap (see photo 4). For a k1-wy2, with only two initial wraps, there will be no drops between the lead and end wraps.

The abbreviation, kw-f/f, is also a single-stitch increase that looks like a knit followed by a knit (see photo 10). It is made by knitting into the leading wrap (see photo 6), dropping wraps up to the last wrap (see photo 7), removing the left-hand needle from the loop, reinserting it through the loop from the back (see photo 8), then knitting into the front of the last wrap (see photo 9). For a k1-wy2, with only two initial wraps, there will be no drops between the lead and end wraps.

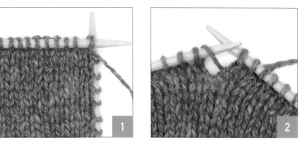

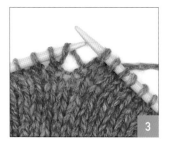

Like many techniques, yarnovers can have multiple applications. Most often used to create the holes you see in lace patterns, yarnovers are also used to increase stitches without holes. Whether you create a hole or not depends on how you work the yarnover on the following row. For a lacy look, follow directions for Open the Yarnover, and for a non-lacy increase, follow Close the Yarnover. Yarnovers created at the beginning of a row can be stacked along an edge and knit later as an alternative to picking up stitches.

Conventional Yarnover

Although this may be the most commonly used way to make yarnovers, there are times when the alternative method is required. Please read notes at the beginning of stitch and pattern instructions to see which method should be used. If a method is not specified, use whichever you prefer.

There are two ways to work this yarnover, and the next stitch to be worked determines how the yarnover is made.

Before a Knit Stitch: If your yarn is not already in front, then bring it to the front between the needles. Carry the yarn over the right-hand needle when you knit the next stitch. The "carry" over the needle is the yarnover, and will be worked either open or closed on the next row.

Before a Purl Stitch. Starting with your yarn in front, carry the yarn over the right-hand needle to the back and between the two needles to return to the front. You have wrapped the yarn around your right-hand needle counterclockwise, one time. Purl the next stitch as usual.

In some patterns you will see instructions to make multiple yarnovers, written as yo2, yo3, yo4, and so on. For these multiple yarnovers, you will wrap the yarn around the right-hand needle one less time than specified. When the yarn is carried over the needle to work the next stitch, the final yo is made. For example, to make a yo3, circle the right-hand needle two times, then carry the yarn over the right-hand needle to work the next stitch.

Alternative Yarnover

Why include this method of making a yarnover and not just the conventional method? It's the way I generally make yarnovers and the way I knit the book samples, but most importantly, it's the only method that works when a yarnover and a short row are worked together on a purl row (as in Folded Cables, page 26). It is also the way yarnovers are made before a p2tog in brioche knitting (see page 175).

Before a Knit Stitch: Starting with your yarn in back, carry the yarn over the right-hand needle to the front and between the two needles to the back, wrapping the yarn around your right-hand needle clockwise, one time. Knit the next stitch as usual.

Yarnovers worked before purl stitches in this book are worked in the conventional manner.

In some patterns you will see instructions to make multiple yarnovers, written as yo2, yo3, yo4, and so on. For these multiple yarnovers, you will follow the same directions as above, but simply circle the right-hand needle as many times as the yo specifies. For example, to make a yo3 before a knit stitch, circle the right-hand needle clockwise three times before working the next stitch.

Beginning of Row Yarnover

These yarnovers, called yo(beg) in the patterns, practically make themselves. It's all about where you hold the yarn when you knit the first stitch. They are used extensively in Linking Hip Sash (page 170) and One-Run Socks (see page 166) in order to avoid picking up stitches that would limit stretch and add an unsightly ridge (see photo 1).

Before a Knit Stitch: Hold yarn to the front and carry it to the back over the needle to knit the first stitch.

Before a Purl Stitch: Hold yarn to the back and carry it forward over the needle to purl the first stitch.

Open the Yarnover

This is worked on the row that follows the making of the yarnover. These yarnovers are worked open to create the holes in your knitting, and are most commonly used in lace patterns, though they may also be used to make buttonholes.

Work up to the yarnover and notice that there is a leading edge to the yarnover. Photo 2 shows the leading edge in front and photo 3 shows the leading edge in back. Knit or purl into the leading edge to create an open yarnover.

Close the Yarnover

To work your yarnover from the previous row and not create a hole, the yarnover must be twisted when it is either knit or purled. To twist the yarnover, knit or purl into the trailing edge of the stitch, not the leading edge (see photos 2 and 3).

Yoc is the acronym for yarnover chain. It is simply a single yarnover followed by a bind-off of the stitch before the yarnover. A single yoc, which looks like a knit stitch, is structurally the same as a single stitch in a crochet chain, therefore a series of yocs is identical to a crochet chain, though the two are produced differently.

For a simple two-step process, the yoc extends the possibilities in knitting. New designs created with the use of yocs are particularly evident in several of the faux crochet stitch patterns. These chains allow you to grow sections vertically, then reconnect with stitches that remain at lower levels. When you wish to work a series of yocs, but do not want to lose a stitch from your pattern when you begin, simply work the last stitch before beginning to yoc with k1-f/b and use the increase for the first link in the chain.

Step 1: Wrap yarn once around the working needle to make a yarnover.

Step 2: Bind off the stitch before the yarnover. For a chain greater than yoc1, the stitch you will subsequently bind off will be the previous yarnover.
Repeat Steps 1 and 2 the number of times equal to the number that appears after the yoc. For example, for yoc8, repeat Steps 1 and 2 eight times (see photo 1).

Abbreviations and Definitions

AO-F: Add on sts, full twist (see Add-On Stitches, page 174).

AO-H: Add on sts, half twist (see Add-On Stitches, page 174).

BO: Bind off

CIRC: Circular

CLOCKWISE: To the right

CO: Cast on

COUNTERCLOCKWISE: To the left

DPN: Double-pointed needle(s)

K: Knit

K1-F/B: Knit into front and back loops of same st to increase one st.

K1-F/B/F: Knit into front, then back, then front loops of same st to increase two sts.

K1-B/F: Knit into back, then front loops of same st to increase one st.

K1-B/F/B: Knit into back, then front, then back loops of same st to increase two sts.

K1-TBL: Knit one st through back loop, twisting st.

K1-WY#: Knit 1 st, wrapping yarn the specified number of times around needle (see Wraps, page 187).

K2TOG: Knit two sts together.

K2TOG-TBL: Knit two sts together through back loops.

K3TOG: Knit three sts together.

KCO: Knitted Cast-On (see page 178)

KW-F/B: Knit into front of first wrap, drop wraps up to last wrap, knit into back of last wrap to increase one st (see Wraps, page 187).

KW-F/F: Knit into front of first wrap, drop wraps up to last wrap, remove left-hand needle from wrap, reinsert in wrap from back, knit into front of wrap to increase one st (see Wraps, page 187).

M1 (MAKE 1 LEFT-SLANTING): With tip of left-hand needle inserted from front to back, lift strand between two needles onto left-hand needle; knit strand through back loop to increase one st.

M1-R (MAKE 1 RIGHT-SLANTING): With tip of left-hand needle inserted from back to front, lift strand between two needles onto left-hand needle; knit strand through front loop to increase one st.

M1-P (MAKE 1 PURLWISE): With tip of left-hand needle inserted from back to front, lift strand between two needles onto left-hand needle; purl strand through front loop to increase one st.

NEXT NEEDLE: The needle following the working needle.

P: Purl

P1-F/B: Purl into front and back loops of same st to increase one st.

P1-B/F: Purl into back and front loops of same st to increase one st.

P1-TBL: Purl one st through back loop, twisting st.

P1-WY#: Purl 1 st, wrapping yarn the specified number of times around needle (see Wraps, page 187).

P2TOG: Purl two sts together.

P2TOG-WY2: Purl two sts together, wrapping yarn twice around needle (see Wraps, page 187).

P3TOG: Purl three sts together.

PM: Place marker

PREVIOUS PEEDLE: The needle preceding the working needle.

PSO (PASS ST OVER): Pass next-to-last st on right-hand needle over last st on needle.

P#SO (PASS # STS OVER): Pass specified number of previous sts over last st on needle.

PSSO (PASS SLIPPED ST OVER): Pass slipped st on right-hand needle over sts indicated in instructions, as in binding off.

PW-F/B: Purl into front of wrap, drop wraps up to last wrap, purl into back of last wrap to increase one st (see Wraps, page 187).

RND: Round

RS: Right side

SKP (SLIP, KNIT, PASS): Slip next st knitwise to right-hand needle, k1, pass slipped st over knit st.

SK2P (DOUBLE DECREASE): Slip next st knitwise to right-hand needle, k2tog, pass slipped st over k2tog.

SM: Slip marker

SSK (SLIP, SLIP, KNIT): Slip next two sts to right-hand needle one at a time as if to knit; return them to left-hand needle one at a time in their new orientation; knit them together through back loops.

SSP (SLIP, SLIP, PURL): Slip next two sts to right-hand needle one at a time as if to knit; return them to left-hand needle one at a time in their new orientation; purl them together through back loops.

ST(S): Stitch(es)

TBL: Through back loop

TFL: Through front loop

TOG: Together

WS: Wrong side

W&T: Wrap and turn (see Short-Row Shaping, page 186).

WORKING NEEDLE: The needle with the attached yarn (working yarn).

WYIB: With yarn in back

WYIF: With yarn in front

YB: Yarn back

YF: Yarn front

YO: Yarnover (see Yarnovers, page 188)

YO#: Work yarnover the number of times specified (see Yarnovers, page 188).

YOC#: [Yo, pso] the specified number of times (see Yarnover Chain, page 189).

Contributors

PAM ALLEN is creative director at Classic Elite Yarns. She is the author of *Knitting for Dummies* and *Scarf Style*, and coauthor of *Color Style* and *Wrap Style*, among other titles.

VÉRONIK AVERY is the author of *Knitting Classic Style*. Her designs have appeared in many publications, including *Interweave Knits* and *Vogue Knitting* magazines and the books *Weekend Knitting* and *Color Style*.
www.veronikavery.com

CAT BORDHI is the author of *New Pathways For Sock Knitters, Book One, Socks Soar on Two Circular Needles, A Treasury of Magical Knitting, A Second Treasury of Magical Knitting*, and the novel *Treasure Forest*.
www.catbordhi.com

WENLAN CHIA is the founder of the fashion/lifestyle company Twinkle and the author of *Twinkle's Big City Knits, Twinkle's Weekend Knits*, and *Twinkle's Town & Country Knits*.
www.twinklebywenlan.com

LILY CHIN has worked in the yarn industry for over 25 years, as a designer, instructor, and author of five books. She has appeared on numerous talk shows, including The Late Show with David Letterman, Martha Stewart, and CNN.

BONNIE DESROCHES loves to knit with yarn spun from her own sheep when not busy creating one-of-a-kind pieces for friends and family. She writes and edits patterns for Peace Fleece.

TEVA DURHAM is the author of *Loop-d-Loop* and *Loop-d-Loop Crochet*. Her yarn line, Loop-d-Loop by Teva Durham, is distributed by Tahki Stacy Charles. Her designs and articles have appeared in all of the major knitting magazines and in numerous books.
www.loop-d-loop.com

NORAH GAUGHAN is the design director for Berroco Yarns and the author of *Knitting Nature*. Her designs have been featured in all of the major knitting periodicals as well as in many books.
www.berroco.com

NANCY MARCHANT moved to the Netherlands from the United States in 1976 and there began a life-long affair with brioche knitting (about which she is writing a book). Her articles and designs have been featured in *Interweave Knits* and *Vogue Knitting*.
www.brioche.com

DEBBIE NEW is an artist and the author of *Unexpected Knitting*. Her life experiences in science, music, electronics, and other crafts challenge her to explore the limits of what can be done with yarn and needles.

ERIC ROBINSON is a musician and adventurer, whose travels often prompt her knitted designs. She is a member of The Green Mountain Spinnery worker/owner cooperative.

LAURA ZUKAITE, a native of Klaipeda, Lithuania, is a graduate of the Parsons School of Design, currently pursuing a career in fashion design and finishing a book of her own designs.

Yarn Sources

ALCHEMY YARNS
www.alchemyyarns.com

ARTYARNS
www.artyarns.com

ATELIER ZITRON
www.atelierzitron.com

SKACEL COLLECTION, INC.
www.skacelknitting.com

BLUE SKY ALPACAS
www.blueskyalpacas.com

BERROCO
www.berroco.com

CLASSIC ELITE YARNS, INC.
www.classiceliteyarns.com

THE FIBRE COMPANY
www.thefibreco.com

FROG TREE YARNS
www.frogtreeyarns.com

GREEN MOUNTAIN SPINNERY
www.spinnery.com

JCA, INC. (Artful Yarns, Reynolds, Paternayan)
978-597-8794

KNIT ONE, CROCHET TOO
www.knitonecrochettoo.com

LILY CHIN SIGNATURE COLLECTION
www.lilychinyarns.com

MALABRIGO YARN
www.malabrigoyarn.com

ROWAN YARNS
www.knitrowan.com

TAHKI - STACY CHARLES, INC.
(Loop-d-Loop by Teva Durham)
www.tahkistacycharles.com

Note: All of the swatches in Reversible Knitting *were worked in Savannah DK from The Fibre Company.*

Acknowledgments

THANK YOU Melanie, because this book began as your idea. Your suggestion for the theme of reversible knitting was intriguing on its own merit, but an additional motivation to work on this book was to see how you would imprint your exceptional sense of style and design on another body of my work. I love all of the STC Craft/Melanie Falick Books and consider it a great honor to be included in the group.

As soon as I started work on this book, I decided to solicit reversible designs from a variety of incredibly talented knitwear designers. Thank you Pam Allen, Véronik Avery, Cat Bordhi, Wenlan Chia, Lily Chin, Bonnie DesRoches, Teva Durham, Norah Gaughan, Nancy Marchant, Debbie New, Eric Robinson, and Laura Zukaite. I greatly appreciate each and every one of your delightful and imaginative designs. Your creations have made this book far richer than I alone could have achieved.

To Jo Ann Luijken (www.wolhalla.nl); friend; author, and lover of knitting in the Netherlands, thank you for contacting Atelier Zitron (www.atelierzitron.com) and arranging for Nancy's yarn.

A giant thank you to technical editor Sue McCain. I am ever grateful for your understanding of the female form in all its glorious shapes and for your inquisitive and pioneering spirit as you edited my stitches and designs. Conversations with you about logic and consistency, while we were creating new abbreviations or seeking simplicity for the reader, were always fun breaks in the solitary hours of designing. And many thanks to JC Briar, the technical editor whose eagle eyes continued to find necessary fixes that have helped us to present a book that we all hope is errata-free.

It's always fun when I finally get to see the work of the production artists – the special people who take all of the fragments and transform them into a useable and visual treat. Thank you Thayer Allison Gowdy and Jasmine Hamed, photographer and photo stylist, for the elegance of your style and vision, and for the clarity of the stitch photos, which are as good as they get when unable to hold the swatches in hand. And thank you to graphic designer Sarah Von Dreele, who with her special artistic flair ingeniously assembled all of the book's various parts.

Thank you Doug for upgrading the little photo studio you built me, for teaching me more about photography, and for always offering support even when I'm unaware that I need it. You are the punctuation to my sentences, the Abbott to my Costello, and you add roots to an otherwise tumbleweed. Even in my search for more clarity while writing knitting instructions you always ask the right questions. You are the greatest armchair knitter I know.